RUSKIN BOND

A CRITICAL EVALUATION

RUSKIN BOND

A CRITICAL EVALUATION

M.P. Sinha
R. Jauhari
Nigam J. Dave

ATLANTIC
PUBLISHERS & DISTRIBUTORS (P) LTD

Published by

ATLANTIC

PUBLISHERS & DISTRIBUTORS (P) LTD

7/22, Ansari Road, Darya Ganj,
New Delhi-110002
Phones : +91-11-40775252, 23273880, 23275880, 23280451
Fax : +91-11-23285873
Web : www.atlanticbooks.com
E-mail : orders@atlanticbooks.com

Branch Office
5, Nallathambi Street, Wallajah Road,
Chennai-600002
Phones : +91-44-64611085, 32413319
E-mail : chennai@atlanticbooks.com

ISBN: 978-81-269-1748-8

Printed in India at Nice Printing Press, A-33/3A, Site-IV, Industrial Area, Sahibabad, Ghaziabad, U.P.

Preface

Ruskin Bond: A Critical Evaluation is, perhaps, the first full length study of the celebrated Indian English novelist and short-story writer. It is rather surprising that in spite of his great popularity and perfect technique, Bond has not been given due recognition by Indian critics whereas novelists of lesser calibre and novels that lack substance have received more honour and admiration than they actually deserve.

The greatness of Bond is that in spite of going back to England, the country of his origin, he decided, like Sir Ronald Ross, to return and settle in India and be a part of its soil. The main reason for doing so was his deep love for his boyhood friends who sustained him with all kinds of support they could during his difficult days. While in England, he could never forget the hilly region of northern India and its people. He learnt from them how to live cheerfully amidst adverse circumstances and how to overcome all kinds of challenges with minimum support. He learnt that it is love and fellow-feeling that are the foundations of the edifice of human society. The young characters in his novels and short stories are all endowed with these two great gifts of nature. His novels, though primarily meant for adolescents, give adults a good idea of the young people's mind and behavioural pattern.

One function of literature is to make us happy, and we certainly become happy in the sunny world of Bond.

We hope this evaluation of the greatest Indian English novelist of the adolescent will help its readers understand his fiction in a new light.

We are thankful to Dr. K.R. Gupta, Honorary Advisor and Mr. Harjeet Singh Publishing Co-ordinator, Atlantic Publishers and Distributors (P) Ltd., for their co-operation.

M.P. Sinha
R. Jauhari
Nigam J. Dave

Contents

1

Introduction

Ruskin Bond (b. 1934) is the most popular Indian English novelist and short-story writer among school children and adolescents. His stories, novels and reminiscences are prescribed in school syllabuses all over India. But it is rather ironical that inspite of his popularity, he has not been taken seriously by critics or even by the reading public. Many writers who write less efficiently than Bond have received more critical attention because they select to write on the themes of communal harmony, social stratification, poverty in India, untouchability or liberation of women. Bond deserves better treatment for his handling of the sensitive issue of "growing up". Young people are the future of a nation. In order to give guidance and direction to youth, their aspirations and frustrations must be understood. It is important to note that a child has tremendous power to grow and fight against the adverse circumstances. Most of the great people have overcome penury and emerged victorious against odd circumstances. Bond's adolescents fight bravely with full optimism and come out with flying colours. He describes their circumstances and helplessness realistically and waves us to the world of the downtrodden and of poverty without being pessimistic. He himself passed through the ordeal of an orphan's life and it is by dint of his hard labour and zest of life, he became a successful writer.

Ruskin Bond's major novels are about adolescents and children. His first novel *The Room on the Roof* is a novel by an adolescent about adolescents. In order that we can better appreciate his novels, it is pertinent to understand the nature of adolescence first.

The term "adolescent" has a specific meaning in psychology. It should not be confused with the word "teenager", although the periods of adolescence and teenage are almost the same. Teenage is the period between thirteen and nineteen. When a boy or girl enters the age of thirteen he or she is called a teenager and continues to be called so till the age of nineteen. The period of adolescence covers the years from thirteen to twenty and according to some psychologists upto twenty-one. However the following chart made by Luella Cole and Irma Nelson Hall is accepted by leading psychologists.[1]

Preadolescence or late childhood	11-12 years (girls) 13-14 years (boys)
Early adolescence	12-14 years (girls) 15-16 years (boys)
Middle adolescence	15-17 years (girls) 17-18 years (boys)
Late adolescence	18-20 years (girls) 19-20 years (boys)

If we look at the characters of Ruskin Bond, all the important characters such as Rusty, Somi, Ranbir, Sudheer, Kishori, Ruth and Suri are in their early adolescence.

The term adolescence is derived from the Latin word adolescere which means "to grow up". According to Lester D. Crow and Alice Crow,

> The period of transition from childhood to adulthood or from dependence on adult direction and protection to self-direction and self-determination is referred to as adolescence, adolescent age or adolescent period of development.[2]

Friedenberg describes adolescence thus:

> Adolescence is the period during which a young person learns who he is, and what he really feels. It is a time in

> which he differentiates himself from the culture; though on the culture's terms. It is the age at which, by becoming a person in his own right, he becomes capable of deeply felt relationships to other individuals, perceived clearly as such.[3]

Adolescence is first of all a period of physical and physiological change. This growth furnishes the basis for emotional, social, intellectual and economic maturity. What are the physical and physiological changes? One may ask. Let us take the physical changes.

The first change in the boys is the growth of hair on face in the form of moustache and beard. Besides hair begins to grow on chest, in the armpit and private parts. The body grows large in size. The growth is so fast that the whole appearance changes at the age of fifteen. Besides, the sweet and shrill voice of the child becomes mature and masculine.

The same case is with girls. There is the growth of hair in the armpit and private parts. The obvious change is the development of breast.

The physiological change is the formation of semen in boys and beginning of menstruation in girls. These changes make them feel that they are growing big and entering a new world, the world of new challenges. This phase, the most important formative phase, is the phase of transition. It is the most important formative phase because, to quote Cole and Hall,

> If a child did not increase his stature, if his muscles did not become strong, if his sex did not grow, if his brain did not mature, if his internal organs did not increase in size and efficiency to meet the requirements of an enlarged body, the child could never achieve mature ideas and attitudes, could never support himself and could never take his place in adult society.[4]

Since adolescence is primarily the stage of development, psychologists have specified the following areas:

1. Physical development—It consists of growth of tissue, muscle, bone and skeleton in totality. Besides there is growth in strength and various skills and physical deviation.

2. Intellectual development—With the enlargement of the brain, there is mental growth. The adolescents begin to show their intellectual abilities and intellectual-cultural interests. In addition they begin to look at things critically and pass their own judgements.

3. Emotional development—Emotion is a response to some kind of stimulus. It is an experience that affects an individual's vital processes, stimulating him to greater activity than is normal. Emotional growth of an adolescent leads him to act with greater drive. His self emerges and he begins to assert his independence and thus there is the development of personality.

4. Social development—The seeds of social development are sown in the family and the primary school. But at a later stage, extra-curricular activities lead the adolescent to have contact with people of all age groups. It is at this stage that boys and girls develop friendship and choose their future career.

5. Moral development—Children do not take religion seriously nor are they sufficiently conscious of the feelings of others. In adolescence, young boys and girls begin to think about religion seriously, the dos and don'ts of society and ethical principles. They accept community influences, sometimes without question and sometimes with a grain of salt.

It is at this stage adolescents think of their goal of life. According to Cole and Hall the main goals of the adolescent are:

(a) Control of emotion by reason
(b) Social adjustment
(c) Independent adulthood
(d) Financial independence
(e) Choosing a career

While pursuing these goals, the adolescent faces a number of problems. It is the responsibility of society to help the adolescent achieve his goals and be a responsible citizen of his country.

We shall study Bond's novels in the light of the findings of eminent psychologists and examine how far he has been able to depict the emotional, moral and social development of his main characters. But before this we shall see some of the novels written by eminent writers where the leading characters are adolescents.

II

If we set aside *Aesop's Fables*, *Panchatantra* and *Arabian Nights* and such Sanskrit romances as *Dasha Kumar Charitam* and *Kadambari*, the first work of juvenile literature is the *Tales of Robinhood*. The world of Robinhood is a free world where the diplomacy and corruption of the court and ill-practices of the so-called holy men are totally absent. It is a world where moral principles (the moral principles of the adolescents) are strictly observed. Even we adults are fascinated by the charm of Robinhood's forest as much as we are by Shakespeare's Arden in *As You Like It*.

The important works where adolescents have leading roles were written in the Victorian era. Dickens's *David Copperfield*, *Oliver Twist* and *Great Expectations* are all great novels but the leading characters—David, Oliver and Pip—are all adolescents. The total career of these characters is a good material for modern psychologists. And so are the two novels of Henry Rider Haggard: *King Solomon's Mines* and *She*. R.L. Stevenson's *The Black Arrow* and *Treasure Island* may be placed in the same category.

Placing these seven novels in the category of novels dealing with adolescence may be called arbitrary by some people. But this is a fact that all the leading characters barring Leo in *She* are adolescents.

When we see him for the first time, David Copperfield is a child living with his mother. His world is the world of innocence and pure bliss. This dreamlike world is broken when Mr. Murdstone and his sister enter it. His trouble begins. His independence is taken away by his stepfather. He is badly beaten by him and, when in self defence, he bites him he is sent to a school where children are badly treated. Later on, he is sent to the blacking factory where his life is very miserable. Unable to bear the hard work and misery, he leaves the factory for his grandmother's home. The journey is painful. He is cheated by the cartman and the pawn broker. By the time he reaches Miss Trotwood's home, he is at his tether's end. All adventures of David are that of an adolescent. He has to work hard for his independence and finance. His problems are those which modern psychologists have listed in our time. David's first problem is adjustment with the new social life after his mother's second marriage. Both he and his mother suffer. The second problem is that of finance. Deprived of all his property he has to work hard for livelihood. At Miss Trotwood's house he receives education. Then there is the problem of love and marriage. Dora makes his life unhappy. Apart from that there is the question of morality. Steerforth betrays Emily in love and Uriah cheats Miss Trotwood in financial dealing. The novel's basic problem is the growth of a child to adulthood.

Oliver Twist, an orphan, suffers like David. Admitted to a private school, he starves. When he demands more food, there is a great astonishment in the dining hall. Later on, he falls in the company of pickpockets and learns the trade. A boy born in a middle class family becomes a pickpocket! He is fed up with that kind of life and wants to escape from the underworld. He runs away but is pursued by Fagin's men. After a lot of encounters, Oliver comes back to his own family and inheritance. The world of *Oliver Twist* is a world infested with criminals. Oliver is surrounded with the evil people and so are other adolescents. The problem Dickens poses is: how will a young boy survive if he is left alone in this dark world? The problems are moral, social and financial.

Great Expectations, too, deals with the life of the adolescent Pip. The novel begins when Pip, an orphan, is a child. His encounter with Magwitch is both horrifying and beneficial. Pip's growth is a gradual understanding of life and world. Romantic in nature and influenced by the glamour of the moneyed class he lives in an illusory world. As a rule his own sister should have been more sympathetic to him but in reality it is Joe Gargery, his brother-in-law who is the real helper. His meeting with Miss Havisham turns his mind. He is dazzled by the glamour of the middle class and wishes to be a member of that society. His meeting with Estella in Miss Havisham's house awakens love in his heart. When he receives money for his education in London, he guesses that Miss Havisham had sent the money incognito.

An adolescent is without experience and rash in judgement. His ideas have their base in heart, not in mind. Pip, in the beginning, is a romantic adolescent. Only after his encounter with the stern realities of the world he becomes wise. He learns that the money he received for his education came from Magwitch, the convict, whom he had given food and the file to get his shackles cut. It is a kind of shock to him that his benefactor is a convict and not the snob lady, Miss Havisham. Estella's rejection is another shock. Pining for a long time in her love, he learns the lessons of life. Joe Gargery's generosity and sympathy bring him back to his own people. Bond's Rusty, too, comes back to his own people after a long wandering. In real life also, Ruskin, one time adolescent, came back to his own people in Garhwal.

Sir Henry Rider Haggard's *King Solomon's Mines* and *She* are not that serious as Dickens's are, but they have adolescents as their main characters. In *Solomon's Mines*, a group of adventurous boys go on an expedition. Since Haggard was racist and imperialist, these adolescents represent more the white people than people in general. There is the search for the valuable treasure of the Biblical King Solomon, which is in the custody of a tribal witch. The boys outwit her but fail to get the treasure. This novel can be called a novel about adolescents but it has nothing to do with the aspirations and problems of teenagers. It is written from the colonial point of view.

She: A History of Adventure is the story of Leo, a young man of the late adolescent period who travels to a remote part of Africa to take revenge on an unknown woman who had murdered his first ancestor, Kallikrates. The scholar Horace Holly, who narrates the story, goes to Africa with Leo. They discover the underground tombs of Kor, ruled over by a mysterious queen who has the secret of eternal life: She—

Who—Must—Be—Obeyed, or Ayesha. She recognizes Leo as the reincarnation of Kallikrates, whom she murdered because he would not accept her love. Leo and Horace are taken to the Place of Life, an underground cavern where they may step into the Fire of Life and be made immortal. When Ayesha herself enters the Fire she becomes immeasurably old and then monkey-like before dying. Shattered and transformed by their experience, the hero sets out for Tibet, where they hope to encounter Ayesha again.

Leo is certainly an adolescent by our standard; he is a ward of Horace. But the novel focuses on the spirit of adventure and the aristocratic ideal of revenge. Though haunting and powerful, the novel does not depict the problems and emotions of the adolescent.

R.L. Stevenson's *The Black Arrow* and *Treasure Island* are about the adolescent life.

The Black Arrow is a pseudohistoric novel. It is set in late 15th century England, during the final stages of the Wars of the Roses. The diffuse plot has three main strands: the first concerns the conflict between Yorkists and Lancastrians, the second the Brotherhood of the Black Arrow, an outlaw band led by John Amend-All (Ellis Duckworth), and the third Richard Shelton, Joanna Sedley, and their relations with his deceitful uncle and guardian, Sir Daniel Brackley. The book ends with Dick and Joanna's marriage and his retreat into private life, abandoning the "heroism" which the novel has exposed as self-seeking and treacherous.

The members of the Brotherhood of the Black Arrow are adolescents, daring, heroic and sacrificing. Their relations among them are ideal as it is usually among adolescents. The growth from romantic heroism to realism is the crux of the novel.

The second novel *Treasure Island* is an adventure novel for the adolescent. Jim Hawkins, the landlady's son at the Admiral Ben Bow inn, acquires a map showing where captain Flint's treasure is buried by Billy Bones, an old pirate hunted by his former confederates. Squire Trelawney and Dr. Livesey Charter a schooner and set sail for Treasure Island with Jim. He discovers that the crew includes the pirates, led by the ship's one-legged cook, Long John Silver. The rest of the story, telling how the pirates are defeated and the treasure found keeps us absorbed till the end of the novel. What is more significant is the character of Long John Silver. Silver embodies every young boy's image of what a pirate should be, courageous, dare-devil, agile and commanding. Jim is the other character to be imitated by adolescents.

Ruskin must have read *Treasure Island* in his school days and the poem "Invictus" by W.E. Henley. It is said that Long John Silver is modelled after Henley. These lines from "Invictus" "I am the master of my fate/ I am the captain of my soul" echo in Ruskin Bond's novels frequently.

Rudyard Kipling's *Captains Courageous* is an adventure stories of three boys who sail a ship and in no sense can it be considered a serious novel worth analysis. His *Kim* is a better novel with its hero of the same name. It is a *bildungsroman*, a novel of development, in which the protagonist, Kimball O'Hara, son of an Irish father and a nurse maid, grows to maturity. Kim becomes an orphan at an early age. He wanders in the streets of Lahore and learns the lessons of life. He learns self-reliance and resourcefulness. He encounters Mahbub Ali who works for the British Secret Service. As an agent of the Secret Service he wanders from place to place, mixes with a variety of people and grows wise. In course of his wanderings as a spy he meets a Tibetan Lama. The Lama teaches him the way how to get rid of the Wheel of Life, in other words, how to achieve *Nirvana*. He does not forget the Buddhist monk and soon follows his path. Later on, he is recognized by the chaplain of his father's old regiment and sent to the school for Anglo-Indian children at Lucknow. He plays an active role in the great game of imperial espionage against the Russians. But, after the total experience of life, he feels that he must travel the path of spirituality. Finally, he goes to the Lama and is united with him at the end of the latter's quest for the sacred River of the Arrow and recites *Om Mane Padme Hum*.

Kim is quite different from the novels we have surveyed so far. Dickens's novels depict the plight of orphan boys in the

Victorian age. The underlying reality beneath exaggeration is easily discernible. We understand the problems of David, Oliver and Pip. We see their progress in life. We admire the way they face the problems. But one thing is certain; they seldom stand by themselves. There is always someone to help them when they are in a critical situation. Haggard and Stevenson are of a different kind. Their protagonists have no social life. They are adventurers. Kim, on the other, represents Kipling's experiences in India. There is no one to save him when he is in crisis.

Kipling's description is realistic. The people in street and the people in train are all Indians, Indians of the nineteenth century. Kim tackles people advoitly but there is no exaggeration. We watch with interest Kim's development. The novel is a great achievement of Kipling. It is a novel about the adolescent, no doubt, but it is much more Kim's journey is at two levels: physical and spiritual.

III

There is a difference between Kipling and Bond. Kipling was born and brought up in India. His early life was spent in Lahore. But he considered himself to be a British citizen, and always maintained a distance and never thought of settling in India. His Kim, a British citizen, is never a true Indian. If we read the works of Kipling we find that he has a divided personality. The conflict between the artist and the imperialist is clearly manifest. He loved India unconsciously but the ideology overpowered him. Inspite of all his sincerity he remained in the group of Haggard, Stevenson, and Henley.

Ruskin Bond stands in sharp contrast. He, too, was born and brought up in India. He went to England to settle there but returned in two years and settled permanently in Mussoorie. In this respect, he is very much like Sir Ronald Ross, the famous doctor, who discovered anopheles and opened the doors of preventive medicines of malaria. He, after a research of about twenty years, told the world that the female anopheles is the propagator of the germs of malaria and scientifically explained the life cycle of the germs. The reason is that he was a humanist, not an imperialist. He loved the sunny climate and the gentle Indian people. Bond, too, is a humanist and great lover of his country which is India. He has never considered himself coming from some other country.

I.A. Richards, T.S. Eliot and the New critics of America are of the view that a writer's biography and interviews are irrelevant matters and a work of art is to be appreciated in its own terms. They are right in their views to a great extent. But it is important to know the causes of the composition—inspiration, contemporary events, literary influences, personal experiences and ideology of the author. We must know why Kipling and Bond are poles apart.

Bond's life-story and journals provide us with the material we need to know: the working of his psyche in the formative years of life. Therefore it is pertinent to make a short survey of his life story and literary influences. This survey will give us a good idea of Bond's milieu and the kind of novels and short-stories he has written. Diana Athill, Andre Deutsch's editor and junior partner, wrote to Bond in 1964:

> Your snag is, surely, that you are a writer who works best from very close to your own experience—which means that one is terribly dependent on the nature of one's experience.[5]

Diana Athill's letter confirms our view that Bond's personal experiences are of utmost value in analysing and interpreting his creative works.

Ruskin Bond was born in 1934 at Kasauli, Himachal Pradesh. His father A.A. Bond had two brothers and one sister. The elder brother Herbert worked as a foreman in the Ishapur Rifle Factory in Bengal. The younger brother Arthur died young and sister Alma died in an air raid in the second world war. Their mother, Bond's grandmother was an orphan brought up in an indigo estate in Motihari, Bihar. Bond does not say anything about his father's occupation till he joined the Royal Air Force nor anything about his mother's parentage. All that he writes about his father's occupation is this:

> (In Jamnagar) My father set up a school room for the palace children. It was on the ground floor of a rambling old palace which had a tower and a room at the top.[6]

He writes about his mother:

> If, in writing this memoir, I appear to be taking my father's side, I suppose it is only human nature for a boy to be loyal to the parent who stands by him, no matter how difficult the circumstances. An eight-year old is bound to resent his mother's liaison with another man. Looking back on my boyhood, I feel sure that my mother must have had her own compulsions, her own views on life and how it should be lived. After all, she had only been eighteen when she had married my father, who was about fifteen years her senior. She and her sisters had been a fun-loving set; they enjoyed going to dances, picnics, parties. She must have found my father too serious, too much of a stay-at-home, happy making the morning butter or sorting through his stamps in the evening. My mother told me later that he was very jealous, keeping her away from other men. And who wouldn't have been jealous? She was young, pretty, vivacious—everyone looked twice at her![7]

This passage reveals three facts. The first is that the marriage was a mis-match. There was a big difference in their age. By Indian standard she was of the age of a niece. Naturally, their mental disposition could not be the same. A man, at the age of thirty-three is serious, business like and ready to bear responsibility. But a girl of eighteen is still an adolescent, hence vivacious and romantic, always willing to go from place to place. The second fact we come to know that she was very beautiful and attracted the eyes of passersby. A.A. Bond, Ruskin's father, was sure to be jealous and would like her to sit with him in presence of others. There may have been quarrels on this matter. The third fact is that Ruskin Bond does not describe her in detail because at the early age of eight he found his mother dallying with some other man than her husband. Later on, we learn that she divorced A.A. Bond and married Mr. Hari, an Indian businessman.

He tells something about his younger sister Ellen, who was physically handicapped. Her photographs are included in *Scenes from a Writer's Life*. This means he had tender love for his sister and retained her photographs till his old age. He writes about her:

> A backward child with defects of vision and the first signs of epilepsy, she had very strong likes and dislikes. For instance, she hated bananas, and if Mrs. Kennedy tried to reason with her by saying, 'Bananas are good for you dear,' bananas would fly about the room and everyone present would have to duck for cover.
>
> Anything that was 'Good for her' was immediately resented and cast aside. Ellen longed to be a bad girl, but she was to retain for all her life the mind of a six-year-old.[8]

However, Ellen was not an idiot or mentally retarded girl; she got a job in a hospital. Coming to his mother again, we find that Ruskin Bond is united again with her after his father's untimely death. At the time of separation she had Ellen and William with her. When Bond met her again there was his half-brother Harold. He lived with her for some time. His step-father accepted him easily and so did his mother. We do not see any complaint against them in Bond's memoirs. But it is certain that no member of his family influenced him deeply nor did he establish an unbreakable bond with them.

It was his father who shaped his life and future career. The first chapter of the *Scenes from a Writer's Life* is about him and his father. He reflects on page 3.

> Not all memories are dream-like and idyllic. I witnessed my parents' quarrels from an early age, and later when they resulted in my mother taking off for unknown destinations (unknown to me), I would feel helpless and insecure. My father's hand was always there, and I held it firmly until it was wrenched away by the angel of death.[9]

The last sentence is significant. There is similarity between David Copperfield's life and Bond's. The only difference is that for the former his mother was the support and for the latter his father. Both lost their support early in life. Secondly, David Copperfield's support was too feeble but Bond's strong enough to make him tread the thorned path of life with full confidence.

With his own experience of quarrelling parents he expresses the opinion that such couples wreck the lives of their children. He writes about his childhood.

> I don't suppose I would have written so much about childhood or even about other children if my own childhood had been all happiness and light. I find that those who have contented, normal childhoods seldom remember much about them; nor do they have much insight into the world of children. Some of us born sensitive. And if, on top of that, we are pulled about in different directions (both emotionally and physically), we might just end up becoming writers.[10]

It is clear from this passage that Bond's childhood was unhappy, the reason being the continual quarrel between his father and mother. He always felt insecure. Like, Dickens, he was a sensitive child. Dickens never pardoned his mother for her insistence that he should continue to work in the blacking factory. Bond, too, did not forgive his mother for divorcing his father and her frivolity. This passage also explains the reason why Bond wrote so much about children. As a child he suffered and, so, developed an insight into their nature and character. He found affinity with Dickens and *David Copperfield* became his most favourite novel.

He writes:

> I was still a pimply adolescent when I decided I wanted to be a writer. I had read Dickens's *David Copperfield* and Hugh Walpole's *Fortitude* and decided that I wanted to be like the writer-heroes of both books.[11]

Great books always influence our lives. The problems of humanity are faithfully portrayed or analysed by great writers and they also give solutions which are supported by their wisdom. The wisdom Bond culled from these books gave him the light to go successfully the dark labyrinth of life. He became an orphan at the age of ten but his determination made him cross all the hurdles of life. At other place in *Scenes from a Writer's Life*, he pays tribute to Dickens and Walpole.

"After *Copperfield* the novel that most influenced me was Hugh Walpole's *Fortitude*, an epic account of another writer in the making. Its opening line still acts as a clarion call when I feel depressed as though I am getting nowhere: It isn't life that matters, but the courage you bring to it."[12]

Books contain ideas but there must be some man to inspire and support a child or adolescent. As quoted earlier the hand that supported all through Bond's childhood was his father. "I learnt to read from my father but not in his classroom", he writes on page 4 of his *Scenes*. He remembers all the details of his life in Jamnagar.

"There were several Englishmen working for the Jam Saheb. The port authority was under Commander Bourne, a retired British naval officer. And a large farm (including a turkey farm) was run for the state by a Welsh couple, the Jenkins. I remember the verandah of the Jenkins home, because the side table was always stacked with copies of the humorous weekly, *Punch*, mailed regularly to them from England. I was too small to read *Punch*, but I liked looking at the drawings.

The Bournes had a son who was at school in England, but he had left his collection of comics behind, and these were passed on to me. Thus I made the acquaintance of Korky the Kat, Tiger Tim, Desperate Dan, Our Wullie and other comic-paper heroes of the late thirties."[13]

This vivid remembrance of books indicate one fact and, that is, Bond became a reader of books right from his childhood. The magazines and comics he saw and read gave him wit and a sense of humour. His humour is manifested in the teaching of Chotu.

"Chotu's reading was slow and laborious, and he paused at every second word, unable to make it out; but there was expression in his voice and, better still, enthusiasm. He rejoiced with the characters of the story and wept when they wept."

"The—Prince—saw—the—Princess—at—the—mouth—of—the—cave! Ruskin, how does a cave have a mouth?"

"Isn't your mouth a sort of opening into your face? So why not call the opening of a cave a mouth?"

"All right... She—had—piles..." He stopped, looked at me quizzically and grinned. "Ruskin, what are piles?"

"Give me the book", I said. "Piles, indeed! I thought as much... She had piles of jewels lying all around her."[14]

Bond's father joined the Royal Air Force in 1940. At that time he was over forty. Bond says:

> He may have bluffed his age (he was born in 1896), but perhaps you could enlist in your mid-forties during the war. He was given the rank of Pilot officer and assigned to the cipher section of Air Headquarters in New Delhi. So there was Bond working in Intelligence long before the fictional James arrived on the scene.[15]

For the first time Ruskin Bond was separated from his parents. His father being in Intelligence was far away. He was admitted to a convent school in Mussoorie. It was a boarding school of the Victorian era, the kind of school criticised in *Oliver Twist*, *David Copperfield* and *Jane Eyre*. Bond reminisces with some humour and some acerbity.

> I hated it from the beginning. The nuns were strict and unsympathetic; the food was awful (stringy meat boiled with pumpkins); the boys were for the most part dull and unfriendly, the girls too subdued; and the latrines were practically unaccessible... I had to endure this place for over a year because my father was being moved around from Calcutta to Delhi to Karachi, and my mother was already engaged in her affair with my future stepfather.[16]

He missed his father very much while studying at Mussoorie. The only solace for him was the picture postcards his father sent to him occasionally. These postcards formed part of Lawson Wood's "Granpop" series—Granpop being an ape of sorts, who indulged in various human activities, such as attending cocktail parties and dancing to Scottish bag-pipes. He enjoyed the postcards greatly and preserved them. He writes:

> I preserved them for fifty years, and now they are being looked after by Dr. Howard Gotlieb in my archives at

> Boston University's Mugar Memorial Library. My own letters can perish, but not those postcards![17]

After the completion of the procedure of divorce, he was taken away by his mother from the school. She did not stop at Dehradun at his grandmother's house; instead she took him straight to the railway station and put the eight year old boy on the night train to Delhi. This action of his mother must have produced revulsion in the young boy's heart. In fact, no mother would do such a thing to her own son. Nobody accompanied him. He was happy to see his father at Delhi railway station.

The two years he spent with his father were the happiest years of his childhood. But his father suffered badly. He became a chronic patient of malaria, the most dreaded disease after tuberculosis in those days, and suffered its bouts frequently. He must have felt it a great burden to rear the self-willed and demanding boy of eight years. But he did his best. He gave his son his time, his companionship and his full attention. When his father was away in his office, he was left alone. Naturally, he had to entertain himself with books, photos and gramophone. This loneliness made him a writer. Besides, it gave him the fortitude to face all difficulties by himself. The life in Delhi, especially when he was living in Sindhia House at Connaught Place, was extremely pleasant for him and, so he resented going to a boarding school.

> When my father broached the subject of sending me to a boarding school, I used every argument I could think of to dissuade him. The convent school was still fresh in my memory and I had no wish to return to any institution remotely resembling it—*certainly not after almost a year of untrammelled freedom and my father's companionship.*[18] (Italics mine)

But after a long discussion, and precisely because his father was being posted at Karachi, he condescended to go to Simla to have a look at Bishop Cotton School. The journey was pleasant and he liked the place. The school, compared to the convent school at Dehradun, was a kind of heaven. He joined the school. The meals served here were of good taste. Life went on happily but soon the thunderbolt came from the blue. His father died! The shock and grief were unbearable to him. The news came to his school. The headmaster entrusted a kind but inept teacher Mr. Murtough with the task of breaking the news to Ruskin.

"He mumbled something about God needing my father more than I did, and of course I knew what had happened and broke down and had to be taken to the infirmary, where I remained for a couple of days. It never made any sense to me why God should have needed my father more than I did, unless of course. He envied my father's stamp collection. If God was Love, why did he have to break up the only loving relationships I'd known so far?"[19]

He retained his father's last letter and it saw the light of the day in *Scenes from a Writer's Life*. He came back to his mother's house during vacations. There he developed friendship with the people both English and Indian. One thing important to note, when we are living in the post-colonial era, is that all the English people living in Dehradun were from the middle or lower middle class living on a low income. Since they had been living for two or three generations they considered India to be their own country and did not hesitate in establishing family relationship with the native people in case they were affluent. Apart from Mrs. Kellner and Mrs. Kennedy, Ruskin developed friendship with the local boys and families.

After vacations, Ruskin went back to Bishop Cotton School, Simla, to complete his studies. He studied a lot of books, especially novels, and played football as goalkeeper. His life there was happy. Here at Bishop Cotton he resolved to be a writer. This was quite natural for an adolescent like Bond. Cole and Hall give their expert opinion on the process of taking decision in the period adolescence.

> The identification by each individual of his own fluid but unique organization is a lifelong process. However, this development seems to reach intensification during adolescence, when the constellation of life experiences, of expanding horizons, of deepening emotions, and of widening social contacts evokes a central need in the adolescent to recognize himself as a whole person, and to

relate himself to other individuals and to the social pattern in which he lives.

> Although this process is actually a complex and virtually indivisible function of the total organism, certain characteristics of it can be observed.... In the simplest terms, this process constitutes a constantly changing balance between his needs and the demands, frustrations, and rewards of his milieu.[20]

Ruskin Bond's personality developed in between hostile circumstances and love and support of the people around him:

> There was Ranbir and his super sister Raj; there was Bhim, already making little business deals; and there were other families in the mohalla, such as the Lals (who became Kapoors in *The Room on the Roof*) and the Sikh boys—Haripal, Dipi, Somi and Chotu....[21]

After his father's influence, the next group of people who shaped his thought process and deepened his love of India are named in the quoted passage. The journals written in 1951 when Ruskin was sixteen-seventeen bear testimony to my argument.

Ruskin made friendship with Haripal, a sikh boy. Later he joined the team that was making an expedition to the Everest. Bond writes about him:

> Haripal, H.P.S. Ahluwalia, grew up to become one of the first Indians to climb Everest. Later, during the Indo-Pak war, he received gunshot wounds which resulted in his being confined to a wheelchair for the rest of his life.[22]

Haripal was introduced to him by Ranbir, one of his earlier friends. In fact Ranbir and Bhim became his friends much earlier and they both helped him when he left his stepfather's house. After quarrelling with his parents (Mr. Hari and his own mother) he left the house and with the help of his friends acquired a room on the roof of the old Gresham Hotel. It is important to describe the entire episode as the room* on the roof of Gresham Hotel

* Ruskin Bond's reference to the place of the room is rather confusing. At first he writes that it was on the roof of Gresham Hotel (93) and now that it was a part of his own house (82). I shall stick to the contents of pp. 82-83.

played an important part in his life and, later on, became a symbol of the adolescent's world in his fiction.

As he was touchy in his teens, he quarrelled with his mother over the radiogram. As he was not allowed to use it for a few days, he missed his favourite BBC comedy show—Much—Binding—in—the—Marsh. The deeper reason behind this trifling matter was his resentment against his stepfather whose business and reputation both were declining fast.

After leaving the house, he found that he could not sleep in the maidan in the winter of late January in Dehradun. So he went to his friend Bhim, son of Dr. Goyal, a year or two younger than him as he had declared recently that he was his "friend, philosopher and guide". He lived up to his declarations and provided him dinner and the small bedroom he had. They spent the night planning Ruskin's future. As he was separated from his parents, he must earn money for his livelihood. The great problem was: How to live till a job is found? Bhim suggested that he should sell his prizes and school books.

> "What about all those books you got as prizes at school," said Bhim. "They are as good as new. We'll sell them at half price to Universal—he'll stick his own bookplate over yours, and sell the lot to the St. Joseph's library."[23]

Ruskin agreed and the deed was done. But the money did not last long. Bhim took his commission and the remaining money was spent in a few days. He had to return to his mother. In the typical adolescent way he announced, without looking if people listened to him, that he would stay till he got a job. Perhaps, his parents did not react to his tantrums and gave him jackfruit curry and rice which he enjoyed heartily. His angry departure had worried his mother and stepfather greatly. So, when he came back home, he was given a separate room. There he felt independence. The description of the room given by Bond is quoted here in full.

> My mother and stepfather took the whole business very calmly, but it must have worried them, because it was soon after this I was given my own room—a tiny *barsati*, opening on to the flat roof of the old building. So it had its own

> entrance and was quite private—except for various birds, squirrels, bats and other small creatures which were also in residence in various corners of that spacious old roof.
>
> A bed, a table and a chair were all that the room contained. It was all I needed—all that any writer needs. Even today, forty-five years later, my room contains the same basic furnishings—only the table is larger, to accommodate more in the way of paper and manuscripts; the bed is slightly more comfortable; and there is a rug on the floor. There is a separate room for my books—a major luxury.
>
> Then, as now, the view from my room, or from its windows, has always been an important factor in my life and in my writing. I don't think I could stay anywhere for long unless there was a window from which to gaze out upon the world.
>
> Of course, I had the entire roof to myself, but the window was important too. It set the scene, so to speak. From my little desk I could look into a bottle-brush tree, and then down the road into the litchi orchard behind old Mrs. Wilson's house—over the trees and rooftops, as far as the far off hills.

Somi, Chotu and Kishen helped Ruskin in making a roof garden. It was the comraderie of Ranbir, his sister Raj, Bhim, Haripal, Kishan, Chotu and above all Somi that developed love in Ruskin's heart for Dehradun and its people.

Haripal invited Ruskin for a lunch. When he reached Haripal's home he was welcomed warmly. Although the entire lunch was prepared by his mother, Haripal boasted.

> I've cooked everything myself, so you have to like it. There is chicken, tandoor ki roti, kulfi...you eat Indian food, don't you? Punjabi cooking is the tastiest in the world though of course, the Bengali will not agree.[24]

As the sweeper's dog had died, the entire family was in the backside of the house, making arrangements for its burial. After sometime Somi, then twelve, burst in and told Haripal and Ruskin that they should dine together as they were all busy with the dog. The three sat together and ate. Somi ate little but pressed Ruskin hard to eat all the items full. Somi's laughter and carefree ways impressed him much. The other thing that impressed him was Somi's garden. It contained "peach and plum trees which were covered with pink and white blossoms. A rich red, flowering bouganvileae creeper climbed the walls, and in front of the house were beds of poppies and marigolds. And there were bees and a swallow-tailed butterfly and sunshine."[25]

Later on, he met Chotu and his mother. Chotu, like Somi, mixed with Ruskin instantly. Their mother was a kind, homely woman with refined features, unexceptional except for a familiar slant of the nose. She was very cordial and her friendliness almost infectious.

Somi advised Ruskin to make a garden on the roof. As narrated in the journal of 15 March 1951, Somi surveyed the whole house by standing on the chimney and then made the plan. Both brothers helped in the making of the garden. Somi went even to the extent of absenting himself from the class. The garden was made. Later on, Haripal introduced Ruskin to Dipi, his cousin who was one year younger. The other boy to be introduced was Dul or Daljeet who joined the Indian Air Force after finishing school. Unfortunately he was killed in a plane crash.

These boys and the neighbours around became an inseparable part of Ruskin Bond's life. A large part of the journals included in his memoir is devoted to Haripal, Somi, Chotu, Ranbir and Raj. Ruskin loved Raj. It was a love of the adolescent and, so, they remained friends, not lovers as the word means.

But as he was determined to become a writer and most of the people said that he could fulfil his dreams only in England, he resolved to go there.

The day of departure came. Earlier he had taken leave of Ranbir and Raj. Haripal, Kishan, Dul and Chotu came to the station to see him off. The engine whistled and after the green flag of the guard started. Somi came running. He drew level with the carriage before the train gathered speed.

"Good bye, Somi!" I shouted.

> "Good bye, Ruskin!" He laughed as he ran, panting, with tears running down his cheeks; and in his voice I recognized the familiar love of fun and life. And don't forget how to laugh![26]

The lessons he learnt in the company of his friends, especially from Somi, remained indelibly printed in his memory. The first is what Somi learnt from a rishi.

> He said, what is the use of collecting money, for when we die we cannot take it with us; and if we have it while we live, then it gives trouble. He said it is unfriendly because everyone wants to be its friend.

And a little later,

> He said, Rich people love money—we, we love life.[27]

The second lesson Ruskin learnt at the time of departure.

> To love and be loved is the greatest happiness.... Men and women leave the age of childhood behind, and are so busy with their buyings and sellings, their ambitions and their hopes, their loves and their hates, that they forget they once lived in a land where dreams were real. I will not forget my childhood. I shall not surrender it.[28]

It was this life in India in general and Dehradun in particular which Ruskin Bond treasured in his heart fondly. Though he went to England and lived among the people of his race, he never forgot the happy years he spent with Somi, Ranbir, Raj, Chotu, Kishen and Kishen's mother.

If Vu-Phuong had responded to his love and agreed to marry him, the turn of life might have been different. Fortunately, for the Indian children, he could not marry Vu-Phuong (unfortunate on his part), returned to India and presented the treasure of children's literature to the millions of Indian people. He gave love and received love.

This brief survey of Bond's early life has been made to understand the reasons why he wrote children's literature and long short-stories, novellas and novels for the adolescent. He himself expresses the view in *Scenes from a Writer's Life*.

> The first twenty-one years of my life form the period covered by this memoir. Although, for most of us, these are not years of great achievement, they are the formative years, and the most emotional, impressionable, vulnerable years. There are struggles, setbacks, failures, but hope and optimism have not been blighted, and the cynicism of middle age is yet far distant.[29]

A creative writer is not a psychologist. Since he faithfully records the feelings, emotions, thought process, cognitive and behavioural pattern of his characters who are taken from real life, he provides a good material to the psychologist to study. Sigmund Freud, when he was praised for the discovery of the unconscious, modestly said that creative writers had already discovered it; all that he did was to give a scientific explanation to it.

Ruskin Bond's novellas and novels depict the life of the adolescents. All the narrations are made by them. No doubt, they encounter the adult world, their perception is that of an adolescent. What is significant is that his novels are based on the real events of his life. Even, at those places where he weaves a fantasy, we clearly see the lurking reality. The second important aspect of his novels and short-stories is the hypnotising narration. He can easily be compared to Chaucer and Dickens. Dickens, of course, has been his model. Like them he is a very absorbing writer.

In the pages that follow his novels and important short-stories are analysed.

NOTES

1. Luella Cole and Irma Nelson Hall, *Psychology of Adolescence* (New York: Holt Rinehart and Winston, Inc, 1966), 4.
2. Lester D. Crow and Alice Crow, *Adolescent Development and Adjustment* (New York: McGraw Hill Book Company, 1965), 4-5.
3. Edger Z. Friedenberg, *The Vanishing Adolescent* (London: Beacon Press, 1959), 9.
4. Luella Cole and Irma Nelson Hall, *Psychology of Adolescence*, 15.
5. *Scenes from a Writer's Life* (Delhi: Penguin, 1997), xii.
6. *Ibid.*, 3.
7. *Ibid.*, 23.

8. *Ibid.*, 49.
9. *Ibid.*, 3.
10. *Ibid.*, 4.
11. *Ibid.*, XV.
12. *Ibid.*, 64.
13. *Ibid.*, 6.
14. *Ibid.*, 103.
15. *Ibid.*, 7.
16. *Idem.*, 7.
17. *Ibid.*, 8.
18. *Ibid.*, 14.
19. *Ibid.*, 30.
20. Cole and Hall, *Psychology of Adolescence*, 267.
21. *Scenes from a Writer's Life*, 90.
22. *Ibid.*, 93*n*.
23. *Ibid.*, 81.
24. *Ibid.*, 95-96.
25. *Ibid.*, 96.
26. *Ibid.*, 129-30.
27. *Ibid.*, 104.
28. *Ibid.*, 130.
29. *Ibid.*, xiv-xv.

2

The Room on the Roof

The Room on the Roof is a novel by an adolescent about the adolescent. The publisher, Andre Deutsch, printed on the dust jacket "an adult novel written by a teenager". Penguin published all the important short stories and novels in one volume in 1996. On the back page of the book it is written.

> In addition to over fifty short stories, the selection includes all the longer works by Ruskin Bond: *The Room on the Roof* and *Vagrants in the Valley*, two classic novels of adolescence.

It is clear that *The Room on the Roof* is a novel dealing with adolescence. As already discussed in the first chapter, adolescence is the period of transition, the period of growth from childhood to youth, a period when all go through a change in body and mind. There is a change in perception from both sides. For the grown up, the adolescent is still a child to be treated in the manner he or she was treated but the adolescent, because of the changes in the body, or what Shaw calls the drive of life force, begins to think and behave in a different way. He or she wants more independence and likes the company of his or her group and shuns the elderly people to whom he or she was closely attached earlier.

Bond has chosen the young boys as main characters in the novel. The reason is obvious. A boy of seventeen could not but write about him and his comrades. The novel is autobiographical, hence true and sincere. While writing it he did not need to read a book on adolescent psychology. All that he wrote is largely a part of his own experience. Some of the characters have the same name they had in actual life. Rusty is Ruskin and Somi is Somi. Some critics may comment that it is not a fiction, it is a life history. May be. But we have to remember that it is a novel by a seventeen-year-old boy, still an apprentice.

Coming to the novel, Bond has put so much in it that we are surprised by its wealth. Let us look at the characters. They are Rusty, Ranbir, Somi, Kishen and Somi's mother. Bond writes in his memoirs:

> After Miss Kellner died there weren't many old people to talk to (not for some time anyway), because I suddenly acquired a number of young friends.
>
> There was Ranbir and his super sister Raj; there was Bhim, already making little business deals; and there were other families in the mohalla, such as the Lals (who became the Kapoors in *The Room on the Roof*) and the Sikh boys Haripal, Dipi, Somi and Chotu....[1]

The room is an actual room. Bond gives a detailed description of the room and how he lived there, in his journals. The following is the entry in the journal of 10th March, 1951:

> I have a new room on the roof.
>
> It stands at the eastern edge of the building and catches the morning sun the same time as the treetops.
>
> The roof is long and flat, made of concrete and I can jump out on it if I like or play a game of rounders.
>
> I am writing in it now, on a level with the birds, an eavesdropper on their conversations. I am high up, a little nearer the stars.
>
> One bold myna, the veteran of many a fight, is sitting on the windowsill and watching me with a furtive eye....
>
> I feel like a monarch....
>
> This room shall be my castle. I shall live in it, write in it, until I must leave it...and I think I shall be happy here.[2]

The description of the room in the novel matches exactly with the passage in the journal. Bond has not deviated even an inch from reality. The passage in the novel,

> It was his first morning in the room, and perched on the windowsill was a small brown and yellow bird, a myna, looking at him with its head cocked to one side. The myna was a common sight, but this one was unusual—it was bald. All the feathers had been knocked off its head in a series of fights.[3]

In the next chapter of the novel he writes:

> In his room, Rusty was a king. His domain was the sky and everything he could see.[4]

If the names and places are real, the experiences, events, emotions and feelings are also real. Rusty's world is the imaginative replica of Ruskin's world.

The novel is autobiographical, not a biography. Rusty is Ruskin to a large extent but not his complete self. The imagined world of *The Room on the Roof* is built on the world of Ruskin, the adolescent and therefore we should analyse it as a novel, not a life-story. Ruskin Bond has mixed fact and fiction as his main aim is to present the emotional life of the adolescent.

It is the story of Rusty, a parentless Anglo-Indian boy in his teenage. His guardian, Mr. John Harrison is a strict Victorian guardian. Typically imperialist in nature and having the pride of the white race superiority over the Indian, he does not want Rusty to mix with them. But, an adolescent that he is, Rusty wants to widen his horizon. An adolescent can never remain confined to the precincts of a bungalow; he must go beyond it and encounter the world outside. This also happens with Rusty. He goes out and meets the Indian people. Being still innocent, not coloured by the white man's prejudices, he makes other adolescents his friends. Though the first encounter is unpleasant (Somi on his bicycle collides with him while eschewing Maharani the ferocious cow) it soon develops into friendship and he is invited to take chaat in the bazaar. He takes it and returns home late. Later on, he becomes a regular visitor.

The festival of Holi comes. His friend Ranbir invites him to play Holi when he is relishing chaat in the shop.

> Rusty was enjoying the chaat. He ate gol-guppa after gol-guppa, until his throat was almost aflame and his stomach burning itself out. He was not very concerned about Holi. He was content with the present, content to enjoy the new-found pleasures of the chaat shop, and said: "Well, I'll see...if my guardian doesn't come back tomorrow, I'll play Holi with you, all right?"[5]

Rusty goes to play Holi with his friends. Had he known the UP style of Holi, he would not have gone to his friends. The treatment he receives there is almost like ragging in a college in a civilized way. He is thoroughly soaked with coloured water and the whole body is smeared with different colours.

> Gently, they rubbed dust on the boy's cheeks, and embraced him; they were so like many flaming demons that Rusty could not distinguish one from the other. But this gentle greeting coming so soon after the stormy bicycle pump attack, bewildered Rusty even more.
>
> Ranbir said: "Now you are one of us, come," and Rusty went with him and the others.[6]

This experience of unlimited joy among his Holi playing changes the whole course of Rusty's life. He feels for the first time the pleasure of independence. Uptill now he had been shackled by the discipline of his guardian, Mr. Harrison.

> He was exhausted now, but he was happy. He wanted this to go on for ever, this day of feverish emotion, this life in another world.... He did not want to go home.[7]

This mingling of Rusty with the Indian boys can be interpreted in many ways. We will all agree with Meena Khorana's interpretation.

> Set in the 1950s, *The Room on the Roof* is a coming-of-age novel that explores the typically adolescent concerns of identity formation, alienation, rebellion against adult

> restrictions, personal autonomy, emerging sexuality, choosing a career, and financial independence.[8]

She is right in saying that Rusty is in search of identity. In support of her argument she quotes the famous psychologists Judith R. Harris and Robert M. Liebert.

> Adolescence is the transitional period from the dependency of childhood to the independence and responsibility of being an adult. At this point in their lives, young people struggle with two fundamental problems: to redefine their relationships with parents and other adults, and to establish themselves as individuals.[9]

But Harris and Liebert are American psychologists and their observations may not be true in the Indian context. Why does the author choose Holi? The answer is that Holi is a festival when all barriers are broken—caste, religion, region and class. People mix freely. They all become alike when smeared with colour. There are no white people nor black people. They are all coloured. Right from the beginning of his life Ruskin Bond, like Sir Ronald Ross, the Nobel Prize winning doctor for discovering the cause of the dreaded disease malaria, loved India, her mountains, rivers, forests and the sunny climate. Mr. Harrison's racial attitude was a great barrier for the growing boy. There are two worlds: the civil lines and the bazaar, the first is inhabited by the former rulers and the second by the native Indians. The bazaar is a prohibited place for the Anglo-Indians. Rusty is warned by his guardian of the consequences of mixing with the Indians, especially the people in the bazaar. But adolescents always want to break the barrier. They have the keen curiosity to see the unknown, experience the things that are novel. Rusty, in his teens, is free from racial prejudices. He does not know why he should remain cut off from the people who inhabit the same land he himself is a part of. The festival Holi is a festival when people forget their caste and class. Colour is thrown on everybody. Everybody is equal on this day. Rusty's playing Holi is symbolic. It breaks the racial barrier. Now he is an Indian.

This mixing with the people of bazaar leads him to love India and Indian people. Somi, Ranbir, Kishen, Chotu, Harpal and other youngsters leave a permanent niche in his mind and heart.

This Holi festival releases him from the bondage of Mr. Harrison. Rusty finds his own self. After his return to his guardian, he finds that he is terribly angry. He is badly beaten for his escapade.

> Rusty stared fascinated at the deep yellow nicotine stains on the fingers of his guardian's hand. Then the wrist moved suddenly and the cane cut across the boy's face like a knife, stabbing and burning into his cheek.
>
> Rusty cried and cowered against the wall; he could feel the blood trickling across his mouth. He looked around desperately for a means of escape, but the man was in front of him, over him, and the wall was behind him.[10]

Not satisfied with inflicting physical pain, he begins to insult him by means of words. The boy listens to him silently in the beginning but soon bursts into anger. He pulls Harrison's legs. Harrison falls down. Then he strikes in the face with a vase. The target is missed but the water and flowers cover his face and he is hit in the side. Not content with this, Rusty holds his collar and slaps his face on both sides. Harrison is injured badly.

This incident which follows the Holi festival is a sequel of the former. Rusty mixes with the Indian people and with their help can break with the dying Anglo-Indian society and live independently. The beating of Harrison gives him the confidence that he can act independently.

> Mad with the pain in his own face, Rusty hit the man again and again, wildly and awkwardly, but with the giddy thrill of knowing he could do it; he was a child no longer, he was nearly seventeen, he was a man. He could inflict pain, that was a wonderful discovery; there was a power in his body—a devil or a god—and he gained confidence in his power; and he was a man![11]

Thus Rusty's departure from Harrison's house can be interpreted on two levels: the leaving of the emaciated Anglo-

Indian society for the healthier Indian society and the departure from the stage of helplessness of a small boy to the stage of strong and energetic manhood.

His new world is free from the oppression of the colonial world; it is a world of freedom, of untrammelled joy and trustful comraderie. This is where the adolescents can developed their faculties in the desired way. Rusty's life can be favourably compared to that of David Copperfield. David lives under the rod of Hardstone. The school is no better and the worst is the Blacking Factory. Unable to bear the murky life at the factory, David runs away. His journey is full of pain and suffering. He is cheated by the cartman. He is cheated by the pawnbroker. It is only when he is at his tether's end that he meets his grandmother, Miss Trotwood, who saves his life. Rusty's life is not so miserable. He leaves Mr. Harrison's house but is never cheated by the people of Garhwal and Dehradun. The people he meets are all simple and sympathetic. Rusty, as said earlier, is partly Bond himself. It was the love of Dehradun's people that brought him back from England and he decided to live in India forever and write about the people here. The sunny atmosphere gives vigour and energy to Rusty. He revives his true spirit.

Leaving his guardian's house, he moves in the streets of the bazaar for a shelter. He sees a house with light. He goes upstairs where he is received well. The woman in the room considers him to be a customer. Her amorous advances trouble him and he leaves the place and sleeps in the open uncomfortably. Next day, it is Somi who takes him home. There he meets his family. After bath and meal, he discusses the future plan. Somi has his mother and two sisters. Though a Sikh by religion he has no ill-feeling for Rusty, a Christian. He considers him to be a member of his family and no one looks at him as a stranger.

The plan is chalked out. Rusty will teach Kishen, son of Mr. Kapoor, a well-off person in the area. Rusty is diffident of his ability as a teacher of English.

> Rusty felt very sceptical about the proposal; he was not sure he could teach English or anything else to the wilful

> son of a rich man. But he was not in a position to pick and choose. Somi mounted his bicycle and rode off to Mr. Kapoor to secure for Rusty the post of Professor of English. When he returned, he seemed pleased with himself, and Rusty's heart sank with the knowledge that he had to go.[12]

This incident in the novel is the displacement of the event in Bond's real life. He writes in *Scenes from a Writer's Life.*

> To give the reader some idea of how I thought and felt and wrote when I was in my seventeenth year, I now give some extracts from the journal I kept in 1951, before leaving for England.
>
> Some of the people described in the journal, such as the Kapoor family, went into my first novel, *The Room on the Roof.*[13]

A little earlier in the same book he wrote:

> There was Ranbir and his super sister Raj; there was Bhim, already making little business deals; and there were other families in the mohalla, such as the Lals (who became the Kapoors in *The Room on the Roof*) and the Sikh boys—Haripal, Dipi, Somi and Chotu....[14]

It is certain that Rusty's adventures are not a pure fantasy. On the other hand, they are real events coloured by imagination or what Shklovsky says made strange by the technique of defamiliarization.

Rusty goes to Kapoor's house. Mr. Kapoor, in his own words:

> ...was once a Big Man himself, and everyone knew this; but he had fallen from the heights, and, until he gave up the bottle, was not likely to reach them again. Everyone felt sorry for his wife, including herself.[15]

He is introduced to Meena, Kapoor's wife and his pupil's mother, Rusty describes her:

> Meena, Kapoor's wife,...was a capable person, still young, a charming hostess; and, in her red sari and white silk

> jacket, her hair plaited and scented with jasmine, she looked beautiful.[16]

The first meeting is rather dry, mechanical and business-like. Meena Kapoor introduces her son Kishen, tells him the terms and conditions of tuition and shows the room on the roof where he was to live. The room is not at all attractive. The author describes it:

> It was a small room, but this did not matter much as there was very little in it: only a string bed, a table, a shelf and a few nails in the wall. In comparison to Rusty's room in his guardian's house, it wasn't even a room: it was four walls, a door and a window.[17]

But the room makes Rusty happy. When Meena says that she will change the room if he did not like it, he replies: "But I like it. This is the room I want to live in. And do you know why Meena? Because it isn't a real room, that's why!"

The room, though very ordinary, is Rusty's citadel. The first reason for liking it is Meena Kapoor. An adolescent, he has fallen in love with her. It is very difficult for us to explain why he fell in love with an elderly lady. As a rule he should have been in love with a girl of his own age or slightly elder. It is equally enigmatic that Meena responds to his love. Strange are the ways of love. But the second reason for his liking the room is that he has got freedom from his guardian. The room is his own and, like Shelley, he can survey everything with the pride of a monarch. The room is a symbol of the adolescent's ideal world—a good company of friends and love of a beautiful woman. Its symbolic meaning is revealed slowly and convincingly.

Now the question is: why did Bond choose the room on the roof, not a small house on the top of a hill or in a lonely island? The answer is obvious. We have to apply Freud's psycho analysis. Freud, in his brilliant essay "Creative Writers and Daydreaming" tells us that when a creative writer finds the real world extremely painful, he escapes into a world of fantasy of which he is the sole master. This world is a kind of child's play. Just as a child derives great pleasure by playing the games of adults, the creative writer recalls the plays or games of his childhood to gain pleasure.[18]

Ruskin Bond does it exactly. In real life, he loses his father at a very young age. His mother has already divorced his father and married a business man. The world for him is dark and wide. He must find a place of solace, a buoy to save him from the hostile waves of life. Somi's family supports him. He is given the room on the roof. The entry in his journal dated 10 March 1951 gives in a good idea of the room. The room in fact was given by Somi's family and he was to teach Chotu, Somi's younger brother. The entire family laboured hard to make the room beautiful and comfortable. Ruskin, too, put a lot of labour in it.

> I have a new room, a room on the roof.
>
> It stands at the eastern edge of the building and catches the morning sun the same time as the treetops.
>
> The roof is long and flat, made of concrete and I can jump out on it if I like or play a game of rounders.
>
> I am writing in it now, on a level with the birds, an eavesdropper on their conversations. I am high up, a little nearer the stars.
>
> One bald myna, the veteran of many a flight, is sitting on the window sill and watching me with a furtive eye. It hops impatiently from one foot to the other but it has no intention of leaving;....
>
> I feel like a monarch. The whole roof is mine, and with it the sun and the stars and the big yellow moon—and yes, that tall tree too, a canopy of scarlet flowers, the blazing flame of the forest.
>
> This room shall be my castle. I shall live in it, write in it, until I must leave it...and I think I shall be happy here.[19]

It is clear that *the room* in the novel is the symbol of Bond's ideas as Byzantium is for W.B. Yeats. The only difference is that Yeats wrote his Byzantium poems in his maturity and Bond the novel in his early youth.

Rusty begins a new life in Kapoor's house; it is a life of fun and frolic and, later on, of growing up. His task is to teach Kishen who is full of mischief and who does not consider him to be his teacher or, at least, does not have that image most children have in their mind. For him, Rusty is a friend. Kishen tricks him the first day. Rusty wakes in the morning but lies still in his cot. He thinks if he should get up and bathe. Then he finds something bump him from under the bed. The whole scene is narrated thus in the novel.

> He (Rusty) stiffened with apprehension. Something was moving beneath him, the mattress rose gently and fell. Could it be a jackal or a wolf that had stolen in through the open door during the night? Rusty trembled, but did not move.... It might be something even more dangerous, the house was close to the jungle...or it might be a thief...but what was there to steal?
>
> Unable to bear the suspense, Rusty brought his fists down on the uneven bump in the quilt, and Kishen sprang out with a cry of pain and astonishment.
>
> He sat on his bottom and cursed Rusty.
>
> "Sorry" said Rusty, "but you frightened me."
>
> "I'm glad, because you hurt me, mister."[20]

Funny indeed! It is not an encounter between a teacher and his pupil but between the elder and the younger brothers.

The teaching period is equally funny. There is no proper teaching at all. There is discussion and then personal queries ending with Kishen's remark.

> "You'll be a terrific writer. You'll be famous.
>
> You'll be a king." And Rusty's retort, "Shut up...."

If Rusty is still a boy in the eyes of Somi, Kishen and Chotu and Haripal, he, in fact, has grown up physically and mentally. This growth of an adolescent can be easily seen in the relationship between Meena and Rusty.

Married in her early teens Meena has had a husband twenty years older than her. In other words, when she was thirteen, her husband was thirty-three, the age of her uncle, if not her father. The future events, mingled with her husband's indifference and indolence, makes her lean to the young English boy of sixteen or seventeen. An adolescent is hungry for everything—food, company, love, sex, adventure, play and reading. Meena's beauty attracts him strongly. He confesses to Kishen:

> "Would you be angry if I said I loved your mother?"[21]

Kishen's reaction is:

> If you love her, he said, "I'm not jealous. But it sounds funny...."[22]

Rusty's love for Mrs. Kapoor is not a baseless fantasy. It was an actual event in Ruskin's life. He writes in *Scenes* that while he was in England he had a poignant memory of India which made him return to India. This poignant memory of the past was relived when he started the novel *The Room on the Roof*.

> Back in the little attic room which I had to myself, I started putting together a novel of sorts, based on the diaries I had kept during that last year in Dehradun. It remained a journal but I began to fill in details, trying to capture the sights, sounds and smells of that little corner of India which I had known so well. And I tried to recreate the nature and character of some of my friends—Somi, Ranbir, Kishen—*and the essence of that calf-love I had felt for Kishen's mother.* (Italics mine)

I have italicized the last part of the last sentence to show the working of an adolescent's psyche. At this stage, there is the development of the body and hence changes in the psyche. Love for the other sex arises at this stage. Peter Blos explains it:

> The aspect of 'being in love' is a more familiar component of adolescent life. It signals the advance of the libido to new objects; this state is marked by a sense of completeness, coupled with a singular self-abandonment. Heterosexual object love brings an end to the bisexual position of previous phases....
>
> To adolescence proper belongs that unique experience, tender love.... He realizes that a sentiment has entered his

> life which is new in one respect, namely that his attitude toward the girl involves a sense of tenderness and devotion. Uppermost are a concern for the preservation of the love object, and a desire for the exclusive—if only spiritual—belonging to each other. The partner does not represent merely a source of sexual pleasure (sex play); rather, she signifies a conglomerate of sacred and precious attributes which strike the boy with awe.[23]

The passage that I have quoted earlier from the *Scenes* tells us that Ruskin Bond wrote diaries or journals. Peter Blos explains why an adolescent keeps and writes diaries or journals.

> Typical for this in-between stage is keeping a diary.
>
> .... The need to keep a diary is inversely proportionate to the opportunity the adolescent has of sharing freely with the environment his emotional urgencies. Daydreams, events, and emotions which cannot be shared with real people are confessed with relief to the diary. The diary thus assumes an object-like quality.
>
> .... The diary stands between daydream and object world, between make-believe and reality, and its content and form change with the times; for material that once was kept as an anxiously guarded secret today is openly expressed.
>
> The older, sophisticated adolescent of today no longer keeps a diary—he writes a "journal". Posterity looks over his shoulder as he writes, however; and what such documents gain in literary quality they usually lose in unselfconsciousness and spontaneity. Diaries today are most frequently kept by adolescents from middleclass families where literary efforts are valued and facility with the written word is not uncommon.[24]

This long passage from America's leading psychologist does not need elaboration. Rusty's character is fully explained by modern psychology and also Ruskin Bond's.

Now coming to the novel's plot again, we see the development of love between Mrs. Kapoor and Rusty. Mr. Kapoor decided to have a picnic. The summer season was approaching. The litchis were almost ready to eat and the mangoes ripened. Kishen liked mangoes very much. In the afternoons, the rays of the sun stole through the branches and leaves of the big bunyan trees and made a pattern of light and shade on the ground and Kapoor's house's walls. The birds knew and so they twittered and chirped in the morning and a lot of noise in the evening when they came home to the tree. In this lusty season the picnic was arranged.

> The car had been inspected, and the two bottles that Kapoor had hidden in the dickey had been found and removed; Kapoor was put into khaki drill trousers and a bush-shirt and pronounced fit to drive; a basket of food and a gramophone were in the dickey. Suri had a camera slung over his shoulders; Kishen was sporting a Gurkha hat; and Rusty had on a thick leather belt reinforced with steel knobs. Meena had dressed in a hurry, and looked like the better for it. And for once, Somi had tied his turban to perfection.[25]

They proceeded on their journey to the picnic spot and made a lot of fun on the way. On the way to the spot Kishen asked Rusty to bathe in the spring of sulphurous water to get rid of his pimples. Rusty jokingly replied that pimples were better than pneumonia. Before reaching the spring they came to a stream. The car stopped in the middle. Kapoor asked the people to push the car. Rusty watched Meena Kapoor roll her sari up to her thighs, and step gingerly into the current. Her legs, so seldom exposed, were very fair in contrast to her feet and arms but they were strong and nimble. Rusty was fascinated.

Evening came. Rusty awoke from sleep. Meena stood in a clearing at the edge of the forest. Rusty went up to Meena, but she wandered into the thicket. He followed her. She showed no surprise as she knew his mind. When they were alone in the thicket, she asked him to listen to the jungle. Rusty replied that he heard nothing. She said that she had meant it and he was to listen to nothing. There was complete silence and they stood motionless. Suddenly, the silence was broken by a piercing shriek, a cry that rose on all sides. Instinctively, Rusty put his arm around Meena. He didn't know whether this act was reflexive of his own fear or Meena's. But he held her tight. Meena asked him why he was so afraid, it was only a bird's cry.

> But he was unable to release his hold, and she made no effort to free herself. She laughed into his face, and her eyes danced in the shadow. But he stifled her laugh with his lips.
>
> It was a clumsy, awkward kiss, but fiercely passionate, and Meena responded, tightening the embrace, returning the fervour of the kiss. They stood together in the shadows, Rusty intoxicated with beauty and sweetness, Meena with freedom and the comfort of being loved.[26]

They stood silent for sometime. Rusty wanted to say something about his love for her in the traditional way. But she silenced him. They looked at a small *cheetal*. The *cheetal* looked at them and stood fixed. Rusty looked at Mrs. Kapoor and then at the deer and found a close similarity. He felt the urge to escape from the town and its people and live in the jungle with Mrs. Kapoor (he always called her Meena), "With no one but Meena." Meena understands his sentiments and says "It would be nice to stay in the jungle." They left the place only when they were alarmed by the snap of a twig.

> The spell was broken, the magic lost. Only the water ran on and life ran on.
>
> "Let's go back," said Meena.
>
> They walked back through the dappled sunlight, swinging their clasped hands like two children who had only just discovered love.[27]

Ruskin Bond does not have deep penetration in the psyche of Meena Kapoor. He presents only one view and that is of Rusty. Rusty is enamoured with her right from the beginning. As the quoted passages from eminent psychologists tell us that sex and love begin with the arrival of puberty and that the energy of childhood is diverted to love of a girl whom the boy admires. Every word, every movement and every reflex charm him. This is all right when both are in adolescence. But Meena

Kapoor and Rusty are quite distant in age. She is in her thirties. She was married at the age of thirteen. Ruskin Bond never tells her age. All that we learn is:

> She was a capable person, still young, a charming hostess; and, in her red sari and white silk jacket, her hair plaited and scented with jasmine, she looked beautiful.[28]

She is a mother of a school-going son. Why should she fall in love with a boy of sixteen or seventeen? We also learn that her husband loves her deeply and, though shorn of his previous glory, possesses still a charming and majestic personality, full of vigour and youth. Therefore, it remains a mystery for the reader why Meena Kapoor developed love for a boy much younger than her, only two years older than Kishen.

This puppy love does not continue for a long time. Meena is killed in a car accident. Kapoor gets an appointment at Delhi. He takes his old car. Meena accompanies him and leaves Kishen in Rusty's custody. But she never reaches Delhi. She is killed in the car accident. A postman delivers the telegram to Rusty who, at first, thinks it to be a letter from his beloved. The death news stuns Rusty and Kishen at first and then they begin to weep. The loss is terrible.

> There was a terrible silence. Kishen looked helplessly at Rusty, his eyes full of tears and bewilderment; and Rusty could stand the strain no longer, and threw his arms around Kishen and wept uncontrollably.[29]

Meena's premature death in the car accident is a turning point in the life of Rusty and Kishen. It creates a wide chasm between the lovely past and the ugly present. The stern reality of Meena Kapoor's death changes Rusty in a moment; he becomes an adult at once, a guardian to advise Kishen, a child. The situation is aggravated by the indifferent attitude of Kishen's father; he shirks his responsibility. The first three pages of chapter sixteen of the novel aptly describe the mental condition of the adolescent and the child. Kishen wanders here and there the whole day and Rusty waits anxiously for him till the evening sets in and stars begin to shine in the sky. He sees the silhouette of Kishen and asks him where he was. Kishen tells him the truth. Rusty is more grieved.

> Kishen slept. He was exhausted—he had been walking all evening, crying his heart out. Rusty lay awake, his eyes wide open, brimming with tears. He did not know if the tears were for himself or for Meena or for Kishen, but they were for someone.
>
> Meena is dead, he told himself, Meena is dead. If there is a god, then God will look after her; if God is Love, then my love will be with her. She loved me. I can see her so clearly, her face speckled with sun and shadow when we kissed in the forest, the black waterfall of her hair, her tired eyes, her feet like jade in the lamplight, she loved me, she was mine....[30]

After this comes the second stream of thought. He is wiser now and also argumentative.

> Rusty was overcome by a feeling of impotence and futility, and of unimportance of life. Every moment, he told himself, every moment someone is born and someone dies, you can count them one, two, three, a birth and a death for every moment...what is this one life in the whole pattern of life, what is this one death but a passing of time.... And if I were to die now, suddenly and without cause, what would happen, would it matter.... We live without knowing why or to what purpose.[31]

Night comes. The howling of a jackal aggravates the fear of their future. The blood-curdling howl of the jackal runs like an electric current through Rusty's body. Kishen springs up with a gasp and throws his arms round Rusty's body. Rusty screams in terror. The jackal runs away. Kishen whimpers and springs back to Rusty. He wraps himself with a blanket and as the scream and its echo dies away, there is complete silence and all that can be heard is Kishen's sobbing under the blanket, terrified not so much by the jackal's howl as by Rusty's own terrible scream. Rusty is equally disturbed by Kishen's sobbing.

If we read the first three pages again, we find that Ruskin Bond has very faithfully portrayed the mental condition and behavioural pattern of the adolescent Rusty and the child Kishen in a critical situation when there is no support. The way Rusty consoles Kishen moves us deeply.

> "Oh, Kishen Bhai," cried Rusty, putting his arms around the boy, "don't cry, please don't cry. You are making me afraid of myself. Don't be afraid, Kishen, Don't make me afraid of myself."[32]

They are like the two lost babes in the woods.

Next morning a tonga comes to take Kishen to his aunt as instructed by his father. As Rusty himself is without support, he cannot retain him. The tonga takes Kishen away. The separation is the cutting of the bond between Rusty and Kishen. For adults, it is the go of the world but for the nascent and sensitive mind of the adolescent it is the parting of the body into two. Even the presence of Kishen's aunt in the tongue fails to give him any kind of solace that Kishen is in protective hands. He thinks:

> I'll go back to my room and time will run on and things will happen but *this* will not happen again...there will still be sun and litchis, and there will be other friends, but there will be no Meena and no Kishen, for our lives have drifted apart.... Kishen and I have been going down the river together, but I have been caught in the reeds and he has been swept onwards; and if I do catch up with him, it will not be the same, it might be sad.... Kishen has gone, and part of my life has gone with him, and inside of me I am all lonely.[33]

While he is in this mood of despair and grief, Somi, his best friend, comes to see him. An embodiment of liveliness, Somi awakes him from the world of grief. As he is deeply grieved, he does not like Somi's humour and his insistence on cucumber.

> Rusty felt irritable. The room was hot, the bed was hot, his blood was hot. Impatiently, he said, "Go and eat your cucumber, I don't want any...."[34]

Hearing his words, Somi stands up and leaves the room before Rusty can say anything. He is so swift in his action that Rusty has no time to recall him. Later on, he shouts but by that time Somi is on his bicycle. He repents for his rudeness. But Somi returns soon. He brings a cucumber for himself and a coconut for his friend Rusty.

This is true friendship. A friend does not quarrel with his friend even if the other has spoken some rude words or made some offensive remarks. Somi understands Rusty well. After drinking coconut, Rusty recovers himself but what is more envigorating is the lively spirit of Somi. Then he says that he is troubled about Kishen. Somi remains silent, munching the cucumber. Then he tells that he is going to Amritsar for a few months and will return in the coming spring. This is another blow. Rusty takes it with difficulty.

> This news was so unexpected that for sometime Rusty could not take it in. The thought had never occurred to him that one day Somi might leave Dehradun, just as Ranbir and Suri and Kishen had done. He could not speak. A sickening heaviness clogged his heart and brain.[35]

Somi watches the change in Rusty's face. He consoles him. They discuss the future of Rusty, an orphan, deprived of home and now forsaken by his friends. He is alone, all alone in the world. Somi asks him in his teenage manner where Rusty wants to go after his departure to Amritsar. Rusty replies that he will go to England. Somi says that it is foolish of him to think of going there when he has no money. His next question is if he is a British subject. Rusty's answer is "I don't know."

His last question is about his birth certificate and when Rusty replies that he does not have any, Somi declares nonchalantly that Rusty does not belong to any place nor is he born in this world.

Their talk, innocent, sad and humorous, leads us to the fundamental problem of race discrimination. For us, all the Britishers were rulers and hated the coloured people. But here, Rusty a British citizen, is an Indian to the core. In spite of his fair colour, he never thinks that he is different from the rest of his Indian friends. All his friends are part of his own self. It follows then that only the high British officers did not mix with the Indian population as we see in E.M. Forster's *A Passage to India* but the common Britishers, who remained in India after 1947, did mix with the native people and established blood relationship.

But as the situation is Rusty must go to England to become a writer and seek a bright future as Ranbir, Kishen and Somi had done by going to Mussoorie, Haridwar and Amritsar respectively. The problem is: how to go there?

He stays at Dehradun. Time passes but nothing happens. After summer, the rainy season, the most spectacular season starts. People revel its arrival. Children go out in the rain to have a kind of shower bath. Rusty's gloom is cleared by the rain as was the dirt of the town, the sky, the earth, the trees and flowers. He, too, bathes in the shower and feels a great happiness. The rain has a better effect than alcohol.

> The rain was more intoxicating than the alcohol, and it was with difficulty that he restrained himself from shouting and dancing in mad abandon. The force and freshness of the rain brought tremendous relief, washed away the stagnation that had been settling on him, poisoning mind and body.[36]

Now the adolescent is changed. Enthusiasm takes the place of morbidity and inaction. An adolescent has tremendous energy in him. A slight hope, a little encouragement or a little support puts him to action like Hanuman in the *Ramayana*. Hanuman remained calm and quiet but when Jambvant reminded him of his prowess, he got ready for action. Rusty also recalls his prowess. He realizes that his life is meant for higher works. He thinks:

> I cannot live like the gardener, the cook and the water-carrier, doing the same task every day of my life. I am not interested in today, I want tomorrow. I cannot live in this same small room all my life, with a family of lizards, living in other people's homes and never having one of my own. I *have* to break away. I want to be either somebody or nobody. I don't want to be anybody.[37]

Rusty's total development can be interpreted in the term of dialectic of the room and the ambition to be a writer of importance. He feels that he will not be of man of eminence if he remains confined to the room. He finds that his friends Somi, Ranbir and Kishen are at other places and his beloved Meena away from this world. The room is, then, a desert, a barren place for him and he must leave it at once. But the great bond of friendship is so strong that he cannot run away from them and the room forever. He has to come back if Somi, Ranbir and Kishen return to Dehradun.

He receives a letter, from Somi, a reply of his own letter, Somi asks him to stay in Dehradun till spring. The letter is quoted in part.

> I know you feel like leaving India and running off to England, but wait till you see me again, all right? You are afraid to die without having done something, you are afraid to die, Rusty, but you have hardly begun to live.
>
> I know you are not happy in Dehradun, and you must be lonely. But wait a little, be patient, and the bad days will pass. We don't know why we live. It is no use trying to know. But we have to live, Rusty, because we really want to. And as long as we want to, we have got to find something to live for, and even die for it.[38]

After reading the letter he folds it carefully and puts it in his shirt pocket. He desire is to keep it forever. It is a letter from his dear friend Somi and contains all his love and wisdom. However, Holi is far away and he cannot remain alone in the room. He must do something for his living and for his ideal. He leaves the room silently. He leaves the door azar so that no one will ask him why he is going away from Dehradun for good.

He decides to go to Delhi and see the High Commissioner for the United Kingdom. He also decides to see Kishen at Haridwar on way to Delhi.

After reaching Dehradun railway station, he buys a ticket of third class, much against the advice of Somi. Luckily, the compartment is not crowded. He takes a seat and waits for the whistle. The train, Haridwar Mail, starts half an hour late, true to the tradition of a branch line. He sleeps on the way. He reaches Haridwar after two hours. He gets down there to see Kishen. He meets first Mrs. Kapoor, a well-mannered lady and asks about Mr. Kapoor and Kishen. She brings Mr. Kapoor. Kapoor is a changed man and looks younger. But what surprises Rusty is his casual attitude to his diceased wife, Meena Kapoor and son, Kishen. He tells that Kishen left the house some time ago and is now living with vagabonds and never comes back home. Kapoor's quick marriage and indifference to his son shocks Rusty. Mrs. Kapoor invites him for a meal but he has become so bitter that he politely refuses the invitation, although he is very hungry.

Kishen has become a delinquent. His father describes him:

> He has been seen along the river and in the bazaar. I don't know where he lives. In a tree, perhaps, or in a temple, or in a brothel. He is somewhere in Haridwar, but exactly where I do not know...no one knows. He speaks to no one and runs from everyone.[39]

Now the question is: why has Kishen, once a sweet tempered boy, changed into a delinquent? Related to this question is Ruskin Bond's portrayal of Kishen whether it is truthful or entirely unreal. Let us take first the definition of a delinquent child. According to the Ohio Code,

> A delinquent child is defined as one who violates a law, is wayward, habitually disobedient or truant, or who behaves in a way that endangers the health or morals of himself or others, or who attempts to enter the marriage relation without the consent of parents or guardian.[40]

This definition matches Kapoor's description of Kishen; Kishen is a delinquent boy. According to L.D. Crow and Alice Crow the most important causes of juvenile delinquency are: (a) lack of supervision by parents and (b) unsettled world conditions. They say that relinquishment by the father of his rightful place as head of the household is a basic cause of delinquency in this country (U.S.A.).

We find in the novel that Mr. Kapoor is rather an irresponsible man. He is lost in the well of wine while his wife, Meena Kapoor, is alive. Her death in the car accident makes no impact on him; he marries early and sends Kishen to his aunt at Haridwar. Cut off from the roots Kishen becomes temperamental and rebellious. The result is that even after the arrival of Mr. Kapoor and his second wife, Kishen remains belligerent and a member of the underworld.

Luella Cole says that:

> Delinquents are sometimes, although not always, emotionally unstable individuals, and they are abnormally sensitive to emotional tensions in their families or neighbourhoods. Unlike the neurotic, who may experience similar feelings, they do not allow themselves to be beaten by the world. They fight back. As a result they become aggressive, hostile, suspicious, jealous, and quarrelsome.[41]

Kishen leaves his home and joins the gang of criminals. His life story is an eye opener to the parents who do not carry out their responsibility and make their home a troubled world.

Rusty goes to the Ganga to have a bath. The cool water refreshes him but when he comes out of the river he finds that all his clothes are missing. He ascends the steps in the same condition, half-naked. Suddenly, he sees Kishen who has been watching him all the time. Kishen did not call him earlier because he did not understand the reason for his friend's presence. But after seeing him alone and almost in a ragged condition, he shouts at him, "Hullo Rusty". Rusty moves forward, his heart pounding with conflicting emotions. Kishen asks him if he is alone. Rusty does not reply but moves upward and reaches Kishen and stares in his face. The condition of Kishen is really bad. The bones portrude from the skin, his hair is knotted and straggly and his eyes dance in all directions searching a lurking enemy. He asks him why he has come to Haridwar and Rusty replies in plain terms that his intention was to see him before his departure from India. Kishen says that he cannot go any where in that weak condition. Rusty sits down on a step and says that he is hungry. Kishen walks into the open and, after approaching a vendor, brings two watermelons. He takes one for himself and gives the other to Rusty. The watermelon quenches his hunger and thirst. He then says that he cannot be a bandit like Kishen because, being a fair complexioned adolescent, he can be easily recognized and caught. Besides, it is not a good thing to be a thief.

Kishen's reply is plain and simple but it reveals the change in his heart, which Rusty's presence has produced.

> I don't rob poor people..., I only rob those who've got something to be robbed. And I don't do it for myself, that's why I'm never caught. People pay me to do their dirty work. Like that, they are safe because they are somewhere else when everything happens, and I am safe because I don't have what I rob, and haven't got a reason for taking it anyway...so it is quite safe. But don't worry, bhai, we will not do it in Dehra, we are too well-known there. Besides, I am tired of running from police.[42]

The mention of Dehra indicates that Kishen wants to leave Haridwar and give up the profession of stealing and robbing. Further, it also indicates that he wants to be in the company of Rusty. Rusty asks him what they will do at Dehra.

> Oh, we will find someone for you to give English lessons. Not one, but many. And I will start a chaat shop.[43]

Hearing these words of Kishen, Rusty forgets everything—England, fame and riches and asks, "When do we go?" Kishen's reply is quicker. He says that they will leave Haridwar next day.

The story of the novel practically ends here. The next chapter narrates their journey in the boat that takes them to the other side of the river.

The novel as we see it is simple in narration and very much traditional in technique. The development of the story is in chronological order. There is little flashback and most of the characters excepting Meena Kapoor and Kishen are types; they remain the same throughout whether Mr. Harrison or Somi or Ranbir or Surie or Mr. Kapoor.

But behind this simplicity of plot and narration there is the complex world of the adolescent, symbolised by *The Room on the Roof*. The period of adolescence as discussed in the first chapter is the most crucial in man's life. Ruskin Bond writes in *Scenes from a Writer's Life:*

> ...these (years) are not years of great achievement, they are the formative years, and the most emotional,

> impressionable, vulnerable years. There are struggles, setbacks, failures, but hope and optimism have not been blighted, and the cynicism of middle age is yet far distant.[44]

The plot of the novel is concerned with Rusty and his friends, all between ten and sixteen. They are carefree adolescents free from the restraints of the adult world and are on the verge of the world of experience. We can say that they are to a great extent characters in William Blake's *Songs of Innocence,* soon to be a part of *Songs of Experience.*

Rusty is a complex character. Born in India of a middle class British, he loses his parents in early childhood. He is under the guardianship of Mr. Harrison who inherits the colonial ideas. The author makes a contrast between the civil lines, inhabited by the bourgeoisie and the bazaar owned by the common people. The adolescent Rusty does not know the reason why he is prohibited by his guardian from going to the bazaar. For Harrison, it is not proper for a Britisher to mix with the common Indian people but for Rusty, the world of the civil lines is a kind of jail where Harrison is the jailor and he must obtain freedom from him and this he does by going to the bazaar and eat *samosa* and *golguppa* at the chaat shop with Haripal, Somi and Ranbir. Unable to bear the tyranny of Harrison, he leaves his house and goes to Somi's for shelter and a new free world. This new world is symbolised by *The Room on the Roof,* a place ordinary, not comfortable, but built by Meena Kapoor, and renovated by Somi, Chotu and Kishen, a world where he is independent of his guardian's sickening influence and where he can dream of his future of becoming a writer of eminence.

His friends encourage him, without knowing the hard path of a successful writer. But this happy room cannot remain happy if its people leave it. It happens. Ranbir and Surie go away from Dehra. Meena Kapoor dies and Somi and Chotu go to Amritsar for a long period and Kishen is sent to his aunt. The room is there inhabited by the lonely Rusty. He decides to go to London.

But when he meets Kishen again and Kishen asks him to return to Dehradun, he forgets his previous decision of going to England. Once his people are with him, he will go back to his world of freedom—the room. Towards the end of the novel, when Rusty and Kishen have crossed the river and entered the forest, Rusty remembers the forest on the day of the picnic, when he had kissed Meena and held her hands and felt the magic of the forest and the magic of Meena. He uncousciously says, "One day we must live in the jungle" to which Kishen replies with a happy laugh.

> One day. But now we walk back. We walk back to the room on the roof! It is our room, we have to go back.

After this follows the authorial comment:

> They had to go back. To bathe at the water-tank and listen to the morning gossip, to sit in the fruit-trees and eat in the chaat shop and perhaps make a garden on the roof; to eat and sleep; to work, to live, to die.[45]

This is the world of the adolescent, a world of untrammelled freedom where they dream of the future and make preparation for the adult life.

NOTES

1. *Scenes from a Writer's Life* (Delhi: Penguin, 1997), 90.
2. *Ibid.*, 99-100.
3. *Collected Fiction: The Room on the Roof*, 600.
4. *Ibid.*, 608.
5. *Ibid.*, 561.
6. *Ibid.*, 568.
7. *Ibid.*, 569.
8. Meena G. Khorana, "The Search for an Identity: Journey as Metaphor" in *The Room on the Roof*, The Creative Contours of Ruskin Bond, P.K. Singh, ed. (Delhi: Pencraft Publications, 1995), 72.
9. *Idem.*
10. *Ibid.*, 571.
11. *Ibid.*, 572.
12. *Ibid.*, 582.
13. *Scenes from a Writer's Life* (Delhi: Penguin, 1997), 92.
14. *Ibid.*, 90.
15. *Collected Fiction*, 583.
16. *Ibid.*, 584.
17. *Ibid.*, 596.

18. Sigmund Freud, "Creative Writers and Daydreaming", *20th Century Criticism: A Reader,* David Lodge, ed. (London: Longman, 1972).
19. *Scenes from a Writer's Life*, 99-100.
20. *Collected Fiction: The Room on the Roof*, 600-01.
21. *Ibid.*, 607.
22. *Scenes from a Writer's Life*, 137-38.
23. Peter Blos, *On Adolescence* (New York: The Free Press of Glencoe, 1963), 100-01.
24. *Ibid.*, 94-95.
25. *Ruskin Bond: Collected Fiction*, 609.
26. *Ibid.*, 613.
27. *Ibid.*, 614.
28. *Ibid.*, 583-84.
29. *Ibid.*, 628.
30. *Ibid.*, 630.
31. *Idem.*, 630.
32. *Ibid.*, 631.
33. *Ibid.*, 632.
34. *Ibid.*, 634.
35. *Ibid.*, 635.
36. *Ibid.*, 641.
37. *Ibid.*, 643.
38. *Ibid.*, 644.
39. *Ibid.*, 653.
40. Quoted by LD Crow and Alice Crow, *Adolescent Development and Adjustment* (New York: McGraw Hill, 1965), 317.
41. Luella Cole, *Psychology of Adolescence*, 426.
42. *Ruskin Bond: Collected Fiction*, 656.
43. *Idem.*, 656.
44. *Scenes from a Writer's Life*, xv.
45. *Ruskin Bond: Collected Fiction*, 660.

3

Vagrants in the Valley

Vagrants in the Valley is the sequel of *The Room on the Roof*. In fact, *The Room on the Roof, Vagrants in the Valley* and *Delhi is Not Far* form a trilogy. Not only the characters but also the story runs through these three novels.

The Room on the Roof ends with Rusty's and Kishen's march toward Dehradun. After crossing the river, they enter a forest. *Vagrants in the Valley* begins with their adventure in the forest while proceeding to Dehradun. Kishen is a changed boy now; the change is from the delinquent to the co-operative. The reason is that he has found in Rusty the father-image which his own father failed to give him. Luella Cole and Irma Nelson Hall write:

> One important long-time effect upon the boys in the family is their deprivation of the customary father image, which usually acts as a model for their own development. If a boy has only a mother or only mother and sisters he has to live in a feminine atmosphere, which may nudge him into delinquencies in his revolt against too many women and his desire to be a *man*.[1]

As the situation is Kishen found in Rusty father-image in *The Room on the Roof* and became a delinquent when he was separated from him. After getting Rusty back again, he is normal and happy as before.

The novel slowly leads us to another room, the church hall, where the adolescents live and where they enjoy full freedom and reign over the land of their heart's desire.

To come back to the plot, we find that Rusty and Kishen who entered the forest in *The Room on the Roof* have crossed it and now are trudging slowly towards Dehradun. Their description links the story of the novel with the former.

> Like Rusty, he (Kishen) was without a home. Rusty had run away from an indifferent guardian a little over a year ago. Kishen had run away from a drunken father. He possessed distant relatives but he preferred the risks and pleasures of vagrancy to the security of living with people he did not know. He had been with Rusty for a year, and his home was by his friend's side. He was Punjabi, Rusty was Anglo-Indian.[2]

While going they discuss their future. As they have twelve rupees in their pocket, they think of selling the things in the room at Dehra. They count the table, the chair, the old tiger-skin a bit eaten by rats, two shirts and trousers. They cannot sell the chair and the table because they are not Rusty's and no one will buy the tiger-skin and the shirts and trousers will be needed by them in future. They are now completely tired. Luckily, they see a bullock cart coming. They board it after making a request to the cart man. But travelling by a bullock cart is not at all comfortable; the cart swings from side to side and they feel that it is rattling their bones. However they reach Raiwala.

After taking a hearty meal for one rupee and six annas, they decide to travel to Dehradun in a midnight train without a ticket. A ticketless journey in a day train is dangerous because they could be caught by the T.T.E. and then put in a jail. They come to the first class waiting room for a rest. Kishen sleeps in an easy chair but Rusty awakes. An American enters the waiting room; he has to go to Delhi by a night train. He sits, takes out a bottle of brandy and two glasses and offers a peg to Rusty. Rusty hesitates first but drinks when the American insists. The brandy has a nourishing effect on him and allows him to speak his mind before the stranger. The cause of vagrancy as stated by him matches well with the findings of modern psychology and sociology.

> I ran away. I ran away from home, nearly a year ago. I had a guardian, an Englishman—my parents died when I was very small—and I lived in his house, in his community, and it was a world of our own and I never went outside it. Then one day in the rain I met Somi. I became his friend and he took me to his home, and to the bazaar, and he showed me India and the world and life itself. My guardian beat me when I came back from the bazaar, and he beat me when I played Holi and came back home drenched in colour. I returned the beating, though, and ran away....

....

> Somi was my good friend, he did a lot for me. He found a boy—Kishen over there—who needed English lessons, and his family took a liking for me and gave me a place to stay. She spent time with me often—I mean the boy's mother—Kishen's mother—and she was sweet and kind to me.

....

> But then they went away. Somi went away, everyone went away. What could I do, but go away too? What could I do when Kishen's mother died, but go away? and if it wasn't for Kishen, I would never have come back. I wouldn't be here now, talking to you, if it wasn't for Kishen.[3]

The question is: what binds the vagrants together? The answer that we find in this long passage is that love is the binding force. A child, if loved by the members of his family, is tied to it fast. When there is some kind of disruption in the order, he becomes a vagrant. He runs to another world as a rebel to the former world but when he finds that there is someone to sympathise and love him, he returns to the former world. Rusty and Kishen both run away but as Kishen finds the father-image (in India elder brothers assume the role of father, when father is absent or no more) he returns to Dehra and Rusty, too, returns because he finds in Kishen his kindred spirit. Once the nucleus is formed other vagrants join them and they live together happily and do not care at all for the heat and dust of life.

The train for the American comes. Now Kishen and Rusty are left alone. They also board a night train but before they reach Dehradun, the T.T.E. comes to their compartment. They slip away through the other door and hide themselves in a maize field. They break three or four corn webs and roast them in the field and satisfy their hunger. Since they do not want to take any risk on a day train, they decide to go from Doiwala to Dehradun on foot. But Dehradun is twelve miles away and they have to travel a path going through the forest. While journeying Rusty thinks of future how to support himself and Kishen and Kishen, too, has the same thoughts. They move on tired and hungry. After sometime, they face a tiger.

> Well, not quite face to face. The tiger was about fifteen yards away from them, occupying the centre of the path. He was as surprised to see the boys as the boys were to see him. He lifted his head, and his tail swished from side to side, but he made no move towards them. The boys stood absolutely still in the middle of the path. They were too astonished to do anything else, which was just as well, because had they run or shouted or shown fear, the tiger might well have been provoked into attacking them. After a moment's hesitation, he crossed the path and disappeared into the forest without so much as a growl.[4]

After the tiger's departure the stupefied boys gain their voice, though they do not move. They talk in a whisper and discuss whether they should go forward or backward. At last, they decide to go forward. They feel a sigh of relief when the forest is far behind. They laugh happily.

Such is the character of adolescence. An adolescent is dashing, has a zest for life and drive to do something extraordinary and forgets all the trials and tribulations once the ordeal is over. So is the case with Rusty and Kishen.

There are three paragraphs in the chapter titled "The Forest Road" which need to be quoted in full to know the Indianisation of Rusty (Rusky = Ruskin Bond).

> Those early years (of Rusty) had been very English and the only Indians he had known were the servants. When he was five, and very proud, he had informed the cook that

> England was ten times as large as India and the cook had believed him.
>
> As he grew older, the forbidden India—the real India of bazaars and temples and sprawling villages—was discovered in bits and pieces; it was only when Rusty made Indian friends for the first time that he discovered it completely. His guardian had not liked his friends or his visits to the bazaars, and they had quarrelled, and Rusty had run away, living for a year with Kishen's family.
>
> At first everything had been different, physically different—wearing Indian clothes, eating Indian food, bathing Indian fashion—and then different in another, more subtle way, which had him thinking differently too. For though he was old enough to have already absorbed certain Western values, he was young enough and flexible enough to be able to adapt himself to his new and unfamiliar environment, and to absorb something of Indian values. He was not conscious of any division of loyalties in himself, but rather of a double inheritance.[5]

Before independence there were two main classes in India: the colonisers and the colonised. The colonisers were the white people who had made India a part of their empires. The French occupied Pondichery and the Portugese Goa but the rest of India was ruled by Britain. The white people maintained a distance as they were the rulers. As Edward Said has discussed in his monumental work *Orientalism* (1976), the colonisers considered the Asians and Africans far inferior to them and made distinction between "we" and "they". Rudyard Kipling, born in India, but settled in Britain advocated the legitimacy of the empire and asserted the supremacy of the white people. In Forster's *A Passage to India* the District Magistrate, the City Magistrate and the Civil Magistrate have the same attitude to the Indian people. The ladies in the party are full of contempt to the natives, though they themselves come from low families. In *Vagrants in the Valley* Rusty's guardian has the same attitude; he beats Rusty for mixing with the people of Dehradun bazaar. He is of the opinion that the English people, being of a superior race, must not be friendly with the common

Indians. Rusty, on the other hand, revolts against this colonial attitude without knowing the world. This is typical of the adolescents that they believe in their friends, love them and feel that they are all tied together with the bond of comraderie. Ruskin Bond, without reading political scientists and sociologists, has thrown light on the colonial attitude of the westerners and the common people's rejection of it.

The two boys move on foot. The danger now passed, they revive their spirit, grow light-hearted and walk into the fertile valley that lies between the Siwaliks and the Himalyan foot hills. At last they came to the bazaar where they take a hearty meal and tea. Now the problem is to have a shelter. At first, they go to the room on the roof. Everything is the same except the people. Rusty remembers Meena and her husband. He finds that the room is locked and the lock is not his but of some other person. Kishen and he see the *munshi* of the *seth* who owns the house and of which Mr. Kapoor was a tenant. The *munshi* tells them that the room is let out and they should go elsewhere. Kishen is in a mood to quarrel but Rusty advises him to leave the place. They come to the tea shop, take tea and listen to the ghost story of the shopkeeper. They offer a glass of tea to the dumb called *Goonga*. Later on, the dumb boy becomes a member of Rusty's group. As there is no place to sleep, they sleep in the open.

Their next adventure is finding a job and a room. Kishen keeps all the nine rupees with him and the remaining four annas are spent on Rusty's shaving. Kishen meets a group of tricksters and loses one rupee in the game. Rusty goes from school to school for a job. Only one school asks him to come after two days. While roaming in the town Rusty reaches the abandoned St. Paul's church. The church is dirty and dark but as it is not possessed by anybody (the padre left it long ago), he decides that he and Kishen will live there together. They meet at the Clock Tower and after that they go for a meal. Though the present is dark and the future is visible, they are not at all despondent. The zest for life is always present in them.

Luckily, they decide to go to Somi's house. They meet his mother, a very kind lady. She gives them a very good meal, inquires about their welfare and asks them to come to her whenever they get time. She also offers them monetary help but they politely decline. Rusty takes Somi's address of Amritsar. After that they buy two candles and go to the church. They keep a candle burning at the door and enter the hall with the help of the other.

Their next adventure is described in the next chapter, "New Encounters".

Kishen does not like the place and wants to stay in Somi's house and the reason he gives for his dislike of the place is that it is very quiet and creepy. But Rusty insists on living in the abandoned church because it is better to sleep there than under trees. In the mean time a bat swoops. Kishen is disturbed and says that a *maidan* is better than that place.

Now Rusty starts writing. This is one important feature of Rusty's personality which comes to light before us. Kishen sits quietly on a bench and does not interrupt him because,

> He knew better than to interrupt when Rusty was writing or reading, particularly so when he was reading. Once Rusty was absorbed in a book, only something disastrous would get him away from it. He had been a bookworm ever since he had learnt to read, but the final commitment had been at the age of twelve.[6]

Rusty's love of books began at the age of twelve when he went with a few hunters on *shikar* into the Terai jungles near Dehradun. The prospect of a week in the jungle, as camp-follower to several egotistic adults with guns, filled him with dismay. Luckily he discovered a shelf of books half-hidden in a corner of the rest house. There were about thirty volumes. The shelf consisted of the works of Charles Dickens, P.G. Wodehouse, M.R. James, George Eliot, Somerset Maugham and James Barrie. He read them avidly as he was all alone in the rest house while the hunters sweated in the jungle and could shoot two miserable underweight wild fowl.

Rusty's encounter with the famous British novelists is a displacement of Ruskin Bond's experience in his actual life. He writes in *Scenes from a Writer's Life*:

The school library—the Anderson library—was fairly stocked, and it was to be something of a heaven for me over the next three years.[7]

And a few pages after page 64, these lines occur:

I was sixteen that year, and I felt I was wasting time in school. Dickens hadn't done much schooling, I reasoned; nor had Jack London, or Joseph Conrad or the Bronte sisters or other favourite authors. I had only to write a book and I would be in their glorious company! I'd been given charge of the Anderson Library, and it became my retreat and my private academy. I worked my way though [sic] the complete plays of George Bernard Shaw and J.M. Barrie, and devoured the novels of H.G. Wells, J.B. Priestley and the short stories of H.E. Bates, William Sarogan (who had recently burst on the scene) and A.E. Coppard.[7a]

Anderson Library has become the bookshelf in the rest house and other writers are named except James Barrie in the novel. Mr. Jones becomes the unknown hunter. Such is the flight of a creative writer's imagination; it takes raw materials of life and transmutes them into a work of art.

In the early hours of the morning a mouse nibbles at Kishen's toes and he awakes with a shriek and shakes Rusty and tells him that he has been bitten by a church mouse. Rusty jokes: "At least it isn't a cathedral rat." He uses the word cathedral because Kishen used the word cathedral for church earlier. However, he comforts him and Kishen sleeps putting his arm round Rusty.

They awake early in the morning and go for a bath in the nearby stream. After bath, they come to the maidan where wrestlers do their exercise and meet Hathi, the strongest wrestler. He is like a young bull, with a magnificent chest, and great broad thighs. His light brown hair and eyes are in startling contrast to the rest of his dark body. He relies more on strength than skill and with a sweep of his broad hand he can level an opponent to the ground. Kishen and Rusty find him at the tap, washing the mud and oil from his body. When he looks up and sees Rusty, he gives a shout of recognition, leaves the tap running and embraces him warmly. The result of the embrace is that Rusty's already soiled shirt is smeared with mud and oil. Then Hathi sees Kishen and saying "And Kishen Bhaiya, how are you?" hugs him. Kishen receives the bear-hug with a grumble and says: "I've already had my bath, Hathi."

In Hindi, the word *hathi* means an elephant and Hathi is an elephant in comparison to his friends and behaves in the like manner. He says that he will go to his village very soon and then invites both of them to come to his place where Rusty can write novels and short-stories. Rusty says that he will go to him after sometime. His present task is to find a job. Kishen goes with Hathi to the bazaar where Hathi has to realize money from the debtors and Rusty goes to the school which had asked him to come in two or three days.

Kishen and Rusty do not know that this separation for a few hours will change into a separation of a long time.

It so happens that while Hathi is engaged in arguing with a man about a certain amount of money, Kishen wanders off on his own. He sees Mrs. Bhushan in a cloth shop and her daughter Aruna of his own age. Because he doesn't like Mrs. Bhushan, he avoids even Aruna and, so, he turns his back on the shop and looks around for Hathi. While he is about to walk away, he feels a heavy hand descend on his shoulder and turning behind he finds the imposing thirty-five years old Mrs. Bhushan, a bullish woman of whom her husband, servants and dogs were equally afraid. The encounter is described in the most humorous way.

> "Kishen!" exclaimed Mrs. Bhushan, pouncing upon the poor boy. "What are you doing here?" And at the same time Aruna saw him, and her green eyes brightened, and she cried, "Kishen! What are you doing here? We thought you were in Haridwar!"
>
> Kishen was confused. To have Mrs. Bhushan towering over him was like experiencing an eclipse of the sun. Moreover, he did not know how to explain his presence in Dehradun. He contented himself with grinning sheepishly at Aruna.[8]

She remonstrates Kishen for his untidy clothes and appearance. She rightly suspects that he has absconded from his father's house at Haridwar. She, much against the will of Kishen, takes him to her old car and drives it fast. The whole scene is so funny that we burst into laughter. The lame beggar's action is really laughter-provoking.

> And she trod on the accelerator with such ferocity that a lame beggar, who had been dawdling in the middle of the road, suddenly regained the use of both legs and sprang nimbly on to the pavement.[9]

Mrs. Bhushan brings him home and asks questions as to how he could be in Dehradun. He narrates everything and she deprecates Rusty as a rogue. But, Aruna on the other hand, likes his adventures. He is asked to have a bath. He bathes with a soap. The rich lather washes all his dirt and his skin glows to its natural colour. Mrs. Bhushan gives him other clothes and throws away the dirty rags he has been wearing till now.

Rusty does not get the job. He wanders in the field. The beauty of the flowers and greenery of the surrounding make him forget everything. He goes on strolling till he reaches the bunglaw of an Englishman whom we later on come to know is Mr. Pettigrew, a friend of Rusty's father. After initial introduction the seventy year old man offers him Solan whisky which gives him warmth and energy. When he tells that Rusty's father was his friend and his guardian Mr. Harrison a bad man, Rusty wants to know more about his father and his whereabouts. Pettigrew tells that he lived with his aunt in the remote corner of Garhwal towards the end of his life and she is the only person who can tell if he left any legacy for Rusty. Rusty thanks him for the information and says that he can go there because one of his friends lives in the nearby village.

Rusty's next adventure is to his aunt's house in the village. But before that he meets Devinder, an orphan Sikh boy studying in Intermediate class and earning money for livelihood and studies by selling combs, plastic toys and other tit bits to people. It so happens that Rusty comes back from the house of Pettigrew and waits for Kishen at the Clock Tower.

Devinder passes by him. They stare at each other for sometime but they do not exchange words. Being tired of waiting for Kishen Rusty comes to the mango tree where he finds Devinder sitting and reading Oliver Goldsmith's *The Traveller*. He asks him about the book. Devinder then says that he is reading it because it is prescribed in the course. Rusty asks about his home and parents. He replies that his parents were killed in the partition period and that he is all alone. Rusty introduces himself and tells that he is also like him. He then invites him to live with him in the church. Rusty finds a greater affinity with him in comparison to Kishen because Kishen's one foot is in the land of the middle class and the other in the land of the homeless people. But Devinder, like him, has both feet in the homeless world. They go to the church.

Kishen is restless. He feels for Rusty because Rusty may be waiting anxiously for him. When night comes, Aruna and her mother sleep, but Kishen remains awake. He enters their room and tells Aruna that he is going to Rusty and be back in the morning.

He sees Devinder and Goonga in the church. He is a bit jealous of Devinder but becomes happy again when Rusty tells him about the Sikh boy. Rusty reads *The Traveller* and both Devinder and Kishen listen to him with understanding and Goonga without understanding. They go to the stream next morning to bathe. They swim but Devinder is an expert. Goonga is an expert in buffalo riding. They come back to the church where they find Mrs. Bhushan with her car. She is rather angry but when she sees Rusty, Goonga and Devinder, she becomes a different woman and asks Kishen very politely to come back home. Kishen is unwilling but Rusty persuades him to go to Mrs. Bhushan's and the reason he gives is that he will go to his aunt in the interiors of Garhwal and if he does not see his aunt both will be stuck there. Kishen agrees.

Now, Rusty makes preparation for going to his aunt in Garhwal. But who will help him in his quest for his aunt? He remembers Hathi. He goes to the maidan and then to the bazaar to find him but learns there that he has already left Dehradun for his village. He is surprised to know that Hathi makes his living by making toys. The toys that are for display in the market are pretty and beautiful. Rusty wonders how the elephant like wrestler could be so artistic.

He and Devinder walk in the market and after sometime reach the residential area where they are greeted by a tall young man, Sudheer, nicknamed Lafunga. Devinder wants to help Rusty with some money that may be needed during the journey to Garhwal and, so, he asks Sudheer to return the money. Sudheer, a loafer that he is, suspects his motives but when he learns that Rusty needs money, he assures Devinder that he will give him the required money.

Sudheer, though educated, belongs to the underworld. He works for a *seth* who sometimes has illegal trading. Born on the border of India before partition, he came in contact with a smuggler, became his assistant but when he was shot dead, Sudheer began to work independently. He has connection with two sex-workers, Hastini and Mrinalini. The first as her name suggests is tall and stout and the second in the same manner is as slender as the stem of a lotus flower. Both love him as he helps them when they are in need. He borrows money occasionally from them but returns only half of the total borrowed amount. This time he goes to them, says some endearing words, makes them jealous of the other and borrows twenty rupees from each.

In the meantime, Rusty goes to Mr. Pettigrew, sits with him and asks him about his father. Mr. Pettigrew tells him that he was a good man, a good player of tennis and that Rusty is just like him. Then he offers him twenty rupees that may sustain him during his journey to his aunt's house. He takes it after persuasion. Devinder gives him the twenty rupees Sudheer has returned to him.

Rusty catches the train to Haridwar in the evening. To his surprise, Sudheer boards the train at Doiwala and drops down at Haridwar before it reaches the station and vanishes in darkness. Two policemen search him at the station and then Rusty realizes that Sudheer, after all, is a thief or criminal in the eyes of police.

Rusty goes from Haridwar to Lansdowne and from there to Hathi's home. The journey from Lansdowne to Hathi's home is arduous in the first but pleasant in the second half. The first half is described thus:

> Rusty had walked fast, because there had been no one to talk to, and no food to be had on the way. But he had met a farmer coming from the opposite direction, and had shared the man's meal. All that the farmer had were some onions and a few chappatis; but Rusty was hungry and he enjoyed the meal. When he had finished, he said goodbye and they went their different ways.
>
> At first he walked along a smooth slippery carpet of pine needles; then the pine trees gave way to oak and rhododendron. It was cool and shady, but after Rusty had done about fifteen miles, the forest ended, the hills became bare and rocky, and the earth the colour of copper. He was thirsty, but there was nothing to drink. His tongue felt thick and furry and he could barely move his lips. All he could do was walk on mechanically, hardly conscious of his surroundings or even of walking.[10]

But after this the journey becomes pleasant.

> When the sun went down, a cool breeze came whispering across the dry grass. And then, as he climbled higher, the grass grew greener, there were trees, water burst from the hill sides in small springs, and birds swooped across the path—bright green parrots, tree-pies and paradise fly catches. He was walking beside a river, above the turbulent water rushing down a narrow gorge.[11]

After reaching Hathi's house he is knocked down by a big dog. Of course, the dog belongs to Hathi. Then comes Hathi, who unaware of his strength, knocks the dog down. The arrival is quite funny. The reception is wonderful. Rusty takes shelter in a cosy room.

Rusty is surprised when he receives a letter from Sudheer. It reads:

> Join me at Lansdowne. I have news of your aunt. We will travel together. I have money for both of us, as I consider you a good investment.[12]

Sudheer Lafunga, it seems, is modelled after Bhim to some extent. Bhim in real life is a friend of Ruskin Bond and helps him sell his old books and takes commission for that. If we read the relationship between Bhim and Bond in *Scenes from a Writer's Life* we will surely see some similarity between fictional Sudheer and real Bhim; both talk of investment.

After reading Sudheer's letter, Rusty comes down to Lansdowne where his friend is waiting. Both move on foot to Rusty's aunt's village. After a long walk, they cross the forest but it becomes dark. Cold is the other problem. Suddenly, they see a few huts at some distance. They go to the house where they see light. Reaching there, they knock at the door and when the man in the house asks them who they are, they reply that they are government officers who have come to survey the area and now want a shelter at night. The man whose name is Ram Singh hesitates but after some pressure allows them to come in.

They are hungry and, so, ask Ram Singh if he has some food to eat. Ram Singh replies that he has the day meal and does not eat anything at night. Seeing that there is nothing to eat, they open a bottle of rum and fill two glasses. Ram Singh sees them opening the bottle and pouring out rum. He cannot resist himself, looks at the liquor with greedy eyes and then says that he has had a bad headache for many days and the red medicine in the bottle will cure him of the sickness. The boys understand everything and then Sudheer tells him:

> Well, this will give you a worse headache, said Sudheer gulping down a mouthful of rum and licking his lips. Besides for people who eat only once a day it is a dangerous stuff.

Soon Ram Singh produces pumpkin and potato and with spices makes curry. They all take curry and drink rum. Some rum is left in the bottle. Ram Singh wants more; so he plays a trick. He starts howling and dancing at midnight. Sudheer and Rusty awake. On being asked what has happened to him, Ram Singh says that he is tormented by a demon. Sudheer understands that he is playing a trick and wants to drink the rum in the bottle. He asks him to open his mouth and, when Ram Singh does so, he pours the remaining rum into his mouth. After drinking the rum Ram Singh says that the demon has gone away. At this Sudheer says that the bottle is empty and, so, the demon must not come again. After this they joke about a wife for Ram Singh and discuss her face, nose, eyes and complexion. Then they ask about the lady who married an Englishman. But Ram Singh expresses his ignorance and says that he has heard of such a woman but has no idea of her where about in recent times. His reply has a disappointing effect on Rusty. Realizing Rusty's grief, Sudheer consoles him like a true friend.

> Forget it, whispered Sudheer. "Forget the dead, forget the past. Trouble your heart no longer. I have enough for both of us, so let us live on it till it is finished, and let us be happy, Rusty, my friend, let us be happy...."
>
> Rusty did not reply, but he held the Lafunga's hand and returned the pressure of his fingers to let him know that he was listening.
>
> "This is only the beginning," said Sudheer, "The world is waiting for us."[13]

His soothing and encouraging words console Rusty and he sleeps peacefully. Sudheer may be a loafer, a person involved in minor criminal acts, but he is not a bad man, at least for the poor and helpless persons. Feeling sympathy for Rusty he is ready to help him with all that he has.

It snows at night and when Rusty wakes and goes outside in the morning, he is delighted to see the beauty of nature. The description is worth quoting.

> The snow lay thick on the ground, carpeting the hillside. There was not a breath of wind; the pine trees stood blanched and still, and a deep silence hung over the forest and the hills.
>
> Rusty did not immediately wake the others. He wanted this all to himself—the snow and the silence and the coming of the sun....

> Towards the horizon, the sky was red. And then the sun came over the hills and struck the snow, and Rusty ran to the top of the hill and stood in the dazzling sunlight, shading his eyes from the glare, taking in the range of mountains and the valley and the stream that cut its way through the snow like a dark trickle of oil.[14]

He wakes Sudheer to enjoy the beautiful scene but Sudheer is not at all interested in the beauty of the snow and he wraps himself in the blanket again and sleeps.

They resume their journey in daytime and soon reach Rusty's aunt's house. They recognized it immediately as it is constructed on the British pattern. They find the gate open but as soon as they reach there, a large Tibetan mastiff arrives there and instead of barking loudly it growls menacingly, Sensing the danger, they draw back swiftly. A young boy, named Vishnu, comes to the gate and asks their whereabouts and the purpose of their coming to the place. They tell everything. The boy withdraws but comes after sometime, ties the dog with a chain and beckons them to come inside. They meet Rusty's aunt. Her age surprises Rusty. After meeting Mr. Pettigrew he imagined his aunt to be over sixty but finds her to be quite young. She is actually forty but as she comes from the higher region of Garhwal she looks not more than thirty-five. She treats them well. The meal is good, the bed comfortable and her hospitality invigorating. She has a hookah beside her and smokes it regularly. Rusty considers her Lady with a hookah. He also smokes it but the smoke is so powerful that tears come to his eyes and he begins to cough. Besides, there is a severe headache. He cannot sleep well whereas Sudheer goes on snoring rhythmically. He comes out and walks outside. He sees his aunt in sari watching him from a distance. She thinks that he is a ghost but after recognizing him, she asks the reason for strolling. He tells the truth. She massages his head and tells a ghost story. Her motherly care induces him to sleep comfortably.

After all she is his own uncle's wife, almost his own mother. She asks him to stay at her house and write books. She shows him the books he read in his childhood: *Alice in*

Wonderland, The Treasure Island and *Mr. Midshipman Easy*. The books remind him of his childhood and he decides to take them with him.

Since he finds that he cannot fulfil his ambition of becoming a good writer in that remote place, he politely declines her offer. Sudheer appears and asks for food. They leave the place after sometime and travel on foot to Rishikesh. Sudheer likes the place because he can operate very easily from Rishikesh and can go to Dehradun and come back to Rishikesh very easily. They walk a few miles and then catch a private bus. There is a heated argument between the bus driver and the passenger behind him on political matters. The bus driver, in the heat of argument, does not see a boulder before him; the result is that the bus dashes against it and then a tree and then stops after getting stuck. The bus driver remains unperturbed as it is something common to him and the passengers think it better to walk on foot to cover the distance of eight miles. Rusty, Sudheer and a businessman Ganpat proceed. Rusty, willing to see a beautiful river, walks fast and enjoys the beauty of nature but Sudheer and Ganpat, both lecherous fellows, talk about women and prostitutes.

Reaching Rishikesh Rusty watches the Ganga and the pilgrims, enjoys the scene and eats sweets. Sudheer, on the contrary, goes to Hastini and Mrinalini to tell them that he is leaving Dehradun because he has cheated the *seth* and for this, may be arrested by police. However, he assures them that he will visit them occasionally. Mrinalini has the problem of loneliness and she badly needs the company of Sudheer but cannot go away from Dehradun because her old mother is too weak and may die soon. She says she is waiting for her death.

Sudheer returns to Rishikesh. Rusty does not recognize him because he is in the garb of a Sadhu. Only when he grins, Rusty recognizes him that he is Sudheer. They sit together and eat apples. While eating, Rusty talks about his future plan:

> I want to give some direction to my life. I want to work, I want to be free, I want to be able to write. I can't wander about the hills and plains with you forever.[15]

The contrast between the two is obvious. Sudheer wants to live a life which has no aim. He is interested in carnal pleasures and to get those pleasures he is ready to rob people of their money and tell a number of lies. Since, Rusty has been a studious boy and read the English classics seriously, he has the aim to be a good writer. Therefore, he cannot go on living the life of a loafer.

However, Sudheer has humanity in him. The parting pains him greatly. He, like Mrinalini, is now tormented by the idea of loneliness. He brightens up when Rusty consoles him by saying that he will visit him occasionally. Coming back to Dehradun, Rusty searches Devinder but he is not available. Then, he decides to go to the pool of water where he enjoyed bathing in the past. He meets there Goonga who is supported well by Devinder. He jumps into the pool and refreshes himself in the cool sweet water. From there he sees Goonga sitting on a rock and grinning at the monkeys. Looking from Goonga to the monkeys and back to the hairy young man Rusty is convinced that Darwin's theory that man has descended from apes is true. Then he reflects on his destination and says that man, being rational, can never be a monkey and should not be a goonga. There are advantages of being human. The advantage is that he can read books and increase his knowledge.

He decides that he will not be a man like Goonga, a speechless fool dependent on people's mercy. He then takes rest and sleeps. When he awakes, he finds someone sitting beside him. At first he thinks him to be Goonga still beside him but when he raises his head and looks up he sees that it is Devinder sitting calmly. They talk as usual and after that Rusty tells him that he is hungry. A practical and self-made young man Devinder replies that he has already bought food for him. While eating Rusty narrates him everything about his journey to his aunt and also that he inherits nothing from his father. His story disappoints Devinder but he gives a very good practical advice to Rusty.

> So there was nothing for you, except a few books. I know money isn't everything, but it's time you had some of it,

> Rusty. How long can you carry on like this? You can't sell combs and buttons like me—you wouldn't know how to. You're a dreamer, a kind of poet, and you can't live on dreams. You don't have rich friends and relatives, like Kishen, to provide intervals of luxury. You're not like Sudheer, able to live on your wits. There's only this aunt of yours in the hills—and you can't spend the rest of your life lost in the mountains like a hermit. It will take you years to become a successful writer. Look at Goldsmith—borrowing money all the time! And you haven't even started yet.[16]

This advice brings the vagrant back to the world of reality. Oliver Goldsmith suffered only for the reason that he remained a vagrant throughout his life and spent money lavishly and in spite of being a very successful writer he was always a spendthrift. Here, Devinder contrasts Rusty with all his friends who are of a different make-up and who come from different backgrounds. Rusty realizes the stern realities of life.

> Already the dream was fading. That's life, thought Rusty. You can't run away from it and survive. You can't be a vagrant forever. You're getting nowhere, so you've got to stop somewhere. Kishen has stopped. He's thrown in his lot with the settled incomes—he had to. Even Mowgli left the wolf-pack to return to his own people. And India was changing. This great formless mass was taking some sort of shape at last. He had to stop now, and find a place for himself, or go forward to disaster.[17]

Now Rusty is a changed adolescent, no more a vagrant in the valley. Kishen is changing, Devinder is already changed and only Sudheer has chosen a wrong path. Rusty decides to go to Mr. Pettigrew. He takes the books from the church to Mr. Pettigrew to keep them in a safe custody. He finds the old man sitting and lost in his own ideas. The words he utters are not meant for Rusty. Rusty suddenly realizes that he himself is entering the adult world. He feels sympathy for his loneliness that has brought dotage at the early age of sixty. He remembers the other lonely person, his aunt, in a secluded corner of the hills and wonders if he will be like them in future.

> It was loneliness again. In a week Rusty had found two lonely people—his aunt and this elderly gentleman, moving slowly through the autumn of their lives. *It was beginning to affect him.* He looked at Mr. Pettigrew and wondered if he would be like that one day—alone not very strong, living in the past, with a bottle of whisky to sustain him through the still, lonely evenings. Rusty had friends—but so had Pettigrew, in his youth. Rusty had books to read, and books to write—but Pettigrew had books, too. Did they make much difference? Weren't there any permanent flesh and blood companions to be found outside the conventions of marriage and business?[18] (Italics mine)

Apart from its significance of revealing the change in the mental set up of an adolescent, the passage tells us about the plight of a single man. Mr. Pettigrew is lonely for two reasons: the first is that he is a single man and the second that being an Englishman he has not come out of his house to mix with the Indian population. Rusty's aunt is lonely because she, too, has no family and stays at her secluded home in the hills. Rusty does not want to suffer their fate. In real life, Ruskin Bond remains a bachelor, (frustration in love prohibited him from matrimonial alliance), but because of his friendship with the Indian families, especially of Somi, Ranbir and Mrs. Lal, decided to have a family. Now, he has a family without a matrimonial alliance, and is loved by all the members as the *paterfamilias.*

Pettigrew is indolent in the beginning but after recognizing Rusty revives wonderfully and discusses his future life. He advises him to go to England where he can make a living and become a successful writer. He is as practical as Devinder. He advises:

> And you want to be a writer. You can't become one overnight, certainly not in India. It will take years of hardwork, and even then—then if you're good—you may not make the reputation that means all the difference between failure and success. In the meantime you've got to make a living at something. And what can you do in India?

> Let's face it, my boy, you've just finished school. There are graduates who can't get jobs.

He quickly reads the working of Rusty's mind and, so, adds that he may come back to India. Whenever he wishes but he can do so only when he is successful in life. If he is not successful in English, he may get a job in New Zealand, Australia, America or Cook Island. At this Rusty asks him why he did not leave India. Pettigrew's answer is:

> For reasons similar to yours. Because I'd lived many years in India and had grown to love the country. But unlike you, I'm at the fag-end of my life. And it's easier to fade away in the hot sun than in the cold winds of Blighty.[19]

Then he looks at the flowers blooming in the marigold, petunia, and bougainvilaea. The wistfulness with which he looks at them indicates how deeply he loves India and her sunny climate. His final words are memorable.

"My journeying's are over", he said. "And yours have just begun."

Rusty takes the decision and takes leave of the old man. Before going to the church, he thinks of seeing Kishen. It is evening now. He sees Kishen and Aruna dancing. He is convinced that Kishen has grown up and now does not need his support.

The novel ends with Rusty's departure for England. A departure from the near and dear is always tearful. But it does not happen with Rusty. Devinder hires a tonga. There is not enough time for the train but the pony goes so slowly that both Rusty and Devinder fear that they may miss the train. When they say so, the tongawallah says something to the pony and the pony starts running very fast and stops only at the station. To Rusty's delight, Kishen is waiting at the station to see him off. Kishen has come to know from the barber who has learnt it from the egg-shop keeper who has been told by Devinder. Kishen complains that he was not told of Rusty's departure for England. Rusty likes his complaint. The train is over-crowded. They go from compartment to compartment and they all look like sardine tins. At last they find that there is one compartment with a few people. Rusty boards it. They come to know that it is a first class compartment but there is no time to change it as the train is already in motion. Both friends bid adieu. They are happy that they have been successful in getting the train and a room in the compartment. Rusty feels it is good. There are no tears nor sad faces.

> He waved to them from the window, and they waved back, smiling and wishing him luck. They were not dismayed at his departure. Rather, they were pleased that Rusty's life had taken a new direction; they were impressed by his good fortune, and they took it for granted that he would come back some day, with money and honours. Such is the optimism of youth.[20]

Rusty meets the American whom he met at Raiwala. The American asks him where he is going and Rusty replies with enthusiasm that he is going to England. He is not at all nervous that he is going to a place where all people are strangers to him. He feels that he can go to all places in the world.

> "I'm going to England", he said, "I am going to Europe and America and Japan and Timbuctoo. I'm going everywhere, and no one can stop me!"[21]

Apparently, the novel is a description of juvenile activities. The people in the shop fool Goonga. Rusty and Kishen search a room and finally settle in an old abandoned church. Devinder, a student of Intermediate, sells combs and buttons for his livelihood and education. He, too, is homeless and begins to live in the church when he becomes Rusty's friend. They all bathe in the river and frolic and fun. Then there is Sudheer, the loafer, educated but a victim of bad habits. He is with those people who live in darkness. He frequents those places where angels fear to tread. We feel that the novel is fantasy, devoid of all kinds of realism. Sudheer's and Rusty's stay in the house of Ram and drinking of rum with curry is equally fantastic.

But behind this fantasy, there is stark realism. The main theme of the novel is the change of a vagrant adolescent to an ambitious and responsible young man. If we read the novel twice, we find that there are four main characters: Rusty,

Devinder, Kishen and Sudheer. We cannot say whether Sudheer is an adolescent like Rusty, Devinder and Kishen. Sudheer, the loafer, is already an experienced young man and his career is almost hardened. Devinder is struggling hard for his existence and future career. Like all adolescents, he is carefree and optimistic and the path he has chosen is the right one. He has become a wise adult at an early age.

The youngest Kishen is wayward. We have seen him in *The Room on the Roof*. Without Rusty's love and protection he would have been another Sudheer in Haridwar. But he, at Dehradun, cannot move in the right direction under Rusty's guidance, the main reason being the elder boy's helplessness. Economically poor Rusty cannot afford for Kishen's education. Luckily Kishen gets Mrs. Bhushan who supports him and educates him. He finds the right path and a good guidance.

Rusty, the main character, is a homeless orphan. His only hope is his aunt. But he cannot stay with her for his whole life and if he does so he cannot fulfil his ambition to be a writer. He must leave the people with whom he has been living. Kipling's Mowgli leaves the wolf-pack although he gets their love and protection. With Pettigrew he fully agrees and follows his and Devinder's advice. Although he does not get anything in his aunt's house, he gets books and one of them is the first edition of *Alice in Wonderland*. Pettigrew tells him that the book, being the first edition, will fetch him five or six hundred pounds, money enough to support him in England. The value of the book can be interpreted in two ways: the first is its material value (it sells for five or six hundred pounds) and the second is its intrinsic value. The best legacy a father can leave for his children is books which will give them knowledge and inspire them to move on to reach higher goals of life.

The novel inspires every adolescent to do something noble and also comraderie and mutual help among their own people. Behind its simple narration, there is the serious theme of the revival of a delinquent to a responsible and healthy adolescent ready to face the challenges of life.

NOTES

1. Cole and Hall, *Adolescence and Social Development*, 428.
2. *Ruskin Bond: Complete Fiction*, 664.
3. *Ibid.*, 668-69.
4. *Ibid.*, 673.
5. *Ibid.*, 675.
6. *Ibid.*, 691.
7. *Scenes from a Writer's Life*, 64.

7a. *Ibid.*, 75.

8. *Ruskin Bond: Complete Fiction*, 695.
9. *Ibid.*, 696.
10. *Ibid.*, 723.
11. *Ibid.*, 723-24.
12. *Ibid.*, 724.
13. *Ibid.*, 730.
14. *Ibid.*, 730-31.
15. *Ibid.*, 749.
16. *Ibid.*, 752-53.
17. *Idem.*, 753.
18. *Ibid.*, 754.
19. *Ibid.*, 757.
20. *Ibid.*, 761.
21. *Ibid.*, 762.

4

Delhi is Not Far

Delhi is Not Far is the story of a struggling novelist of twenty-five years. The title is a variation of the famous words of the Muslim saint who told the king of Delhi that *Dilli door ast* (Delhi is far away) and it is said that the king never reached Delhi. Here the title means that the goal is not far however distant it may appear to be, that is, the goal is reachable and the struggler must not be disheartened by the hostile circumstances.

This novel completes the trilogy. Though the name of the narrator is not given but all his characteristics and struggle to be a writer of fame are convincing evidence of his being Rusty, the main character in *The Room on the Roof* and *Vagrants in the Valley*. Besides, there is a similarity between Devinder of *Vagrants in the Valley* and Suraj of *Delhi is Not Far;* both sell combs and buttons in a tray. Similarly Mrinalini appears as Kamla; both are short-sized delicate figures but expert in sexual games.

The novel does not begin in the traditional way like *The Room on the Roof* and *Vagrants in the Valley,* where the narrator is a third person who observes everything sometimes from outside and sometimes from inside. Here the narrator is the protagonist and all that he narrates is in the tradition of confessional poetry; nothing is inhibited and the conscious and the unconscious play together in day time. It is not even daydreaming nor the confession of guilt before the church priest.

In the opening pages, the narrator describes the town, his room and the people; the technique is quite modern:

"My balcony is my window on the world.

The room has one window, a square hole in the wall crossed by three iron bars.

The view from it is a restricted one. If I crane my neck sideways and put my nose to the bars, I can see the extremeties of the building; below, a narrow courtyard where children—the children of all classes of people—play together. It is only when they are older that they become conscious of the barriers of class and caste."[1]

The beginning is dramatic and the speaker, an experienced, wise and sagacious person. The last sentence is a sad comment on social stratification in India. The time when Ruskin Bond wrote this sentence, the ugly face of class and caste were still hidden but now we see it with dismay and sorrow. The irony in the passage will be clear if we link the last sentence with the previous one. Children have no idea of class and caste; they play together, laugh together and spend their happiest moments together but when they grow up they find themself in different plots fenced with turnpikes.

The use of the phrase "window on the world" reminds us of Robert Lynd's famous essay "Window View". The world is real when we walk on road or in a field or lawn but it becomes a magic world when we view it through a window. We observe everything with great attention and all activities of the people charm us; we look through the looking glass of Alice. The narrator watches the world around him from the balcony which is a window on the Pipalnagar, a small town.

"The room" is Rusty's haven in the previous novels and here, too, it occupies the central place in the narrator's life. It is described:

> My room is very small. I have paced about in it so often that I know its exact measurements. My foot, from heel to toe, is eleven inches. That makes the room just over fifteen feet in length; when I measure the last foot, my toes turn

> up against the wall. In breadth, the room is exactly eight feet.[2]

Then the narrator introduces himself that he is a writer and writes cheap novels and short-stories in English, Urdu and Hindi; the reason for having command of three languages is that he was born in a Hindu family and brought up in Muslim city and educated in an English medium school. His two books fetch two hundred rupees each; a flat and final payment, no royalties. His publisher from Meerut says that he should write a good novel, not detective ones because they have a very limited market. The publisher's remarks on the reading habit of the younger generation is harshly true; they read only to pass examination, not to gain knowledge. The result is a disaster in their future career.

> They pass their exams and then fall by the wayside. The point is, millions are sitting for exams, for M.A., B.Sc., Ph.D., and other degrees. They all want to get their degrees the easy way, without reading too many books or attending more than half a dozen lectures—and that's where a smart person like you comes in! Why should they wade through five volumes of political history when they can get a dozen model answer-papers? They are seldom wrong, the guess-papers. All you have to do is make friends with someone on the University Board, write your papers, print them cheaply—never mind a few printing errors—and flood the market. They'll sell like hot cakes "he concluded, using an English expression."[3]

The first two pages of the novel describe the world as it is, the real world where the narrator lives and where he has to make a living and build his future career and thus it sets the goal for the protagonist. The rest of the pages tell us his struggle against the temptations of the romantic world of adolescents and vagrants.

He is, like most of the creative writers, a poor young man of twenty-five and lives in a shabby room and sleeps on a *Charpai* (stringed cot) under which he keeps his tin box. As there is no private latrine of his and the public latrine near the station is horribly dirty, he goes across the railway line early in the morning, a pitiable life by our modern standard. He goes to the barber Deep Chand, a short thick-set man, to get his beard shaved once a week.

Deep Chand, while shaving his beard, asks him when he is going to marry; he replies that he will do it in five or ten years. Deep Chand warns him that he should not think of five years because by that time he will be old by the Pipalnagar standard. After shaving, while Deep Chand is massaging his head, he goes on calculating how much money he owes to others and others owe how much to him. But one thing is clear: he has to pay Seth Govind Ram, the landlord, six month's rent, sixty rupees.

Seth Govind Ram, one of the richest persons in the town, has a bank, a paunch and a mistress. The first two are visible but the third is hidden from the sight of the people. Few people have seen his mistress. She is kept hidden away in a big house of Rajput-style outside the city and, the narrator says, continues to be a challenge to his imagination.

The protagonist has been an unsuccessful businessman only because he is a dreamer. First, he started a vegetable shop which made him bankrupt. Then came his imaginary tea stall that, too, became a flop. The third was the profession of a palmist. Unfortunately no one came to him. Now the only method to be a man of fortune is to marry a wealthy woman as suggested by Deep Chand. He asks how he can get a wealthy widow. Pat comes the reply that he need not search a widow; the best thing is to find out a fat aged businessman (*seth*) and his young wife. She will support him. A good joke indeed!

The other young people whom he meets are Ramu, Deep Chand's younger brother, Aziz and Suraj, an epileptic vendor of combs and buttons, who studies in a school. There is poverty all around him. People live in single rooms. A family consisting of father, mother and a good number of children, lives in a single room which is used for cooking, eating, sleeping and love making. There is no proper education nor the will to get rid of the marsh of poverty. People seem to have resigned to their fate.

> In Pipalnagar there is not exactly despair, but resignation, an indifference to both living and dying. The town is almost truly reflected in the Pipalnagar Home, where in an open courtyard surrounded by mud walls a score of mental patients wander about, listless and bored. One man jabbers excitedly, but most of the inmates are quite sad and resentful—resentful because we do not try to understand their beautiful insane world.[4]

After this realistic description of life, the author focuses attention on sex in adolescent and post-adolescent periods. He writes:

> At a certain age a boy is like young wheat, growing, healthy, on the verge of manhood. His eyes are alive, his mind quick, his gestures confident, you cannot mistake him.
>
> This is the most fascinating age, when a boy becomes a man—it is interesting both physically and mentally. The growth of the boy's hair, the toning of the muscles, the consciousness of growing and changing and maturing—never again will there be so much change and development in so short a period of time. The body exudes virility, is full of currents and counter-currents.
>
> For a girl, puberty is a frightening age when alarming things begin to happen in her body. For a boy it is an age of self-assertion, of a growing confidence in himself and in his attitude to the world. His physical changes are a source of happiness and pride.[5]

It is difficult to agree entirely with this view of Bond though this novel largely exemplifies it. What he misses here is the value of education. An illiterate or uneducated person, because he does not understand fully the world around her or him, is always apprehensive of the strangers and finds it difficult to cope with the situations that are new. Secondly, his observation on girls is partly true. They wonder at the change and do not like the periodical menstruation but this does not mean that they are scared of the changes in the body; they have already seen the changes in their elders and discussed them.

Mothers, elder sisters and bhabhis are always there to help them and explain the nature of changes.

According to psychologists, the changes in the body bring about changes in the thought process of the adolescent. Sex is there but a small child is not aware of it. The formation of semen and its ejaculation make the adolescent aware of the pleasures of sex. Similarly, menstruation makes girls aware that they can be mothers. Secondly, there is the desire to come near to the opposite sex and have physical contact. Then again, in absence of proper sex education, youngsters play the game like animals.

Although Bond does not state these facts in his generalised remarks, the activities of Suraj, the narrator and other characters reveal this fact of life of the orphans or guardian less teenagers.

It so happens that the narrator, while walking through the fields beyond the railway tracks, sees a young boy lying unconscious among the wheat plants. At first, he thinks that he might have been robbed and beaten badly. So he decides to run away but on second thought he deprecates his own cowardice and goes to him. He finds that the boy has had an attack of epilepsy and is now reviving slowly. He goes to him and helps him in the revival. The boy whose name is Suraj, tells his story that he lost his parents at the young age of five on the railway platform of Amritsar while coming from West Punjab after India's partition.

He is a thin boy, long-limbed and bony. There is a little fluff on his cheeks and a thin line of coming moustache. His eyes hold a secret and mouth a hesitant smile. He tells the narrator that he is a student of Pipalnagar college and his terminal examination will be held in August. If he passes the examination, he will get scholarship and have a bright future, otherwise a dull life and the profession of selling combs, buttons and vials of perfume. As he is homeless, he is offered the room to share with the narrator.

Later on, Suraj comes to his room and sleeps at the top of the steps. The narrator shakes him gently and asks him why he did not come into the room. Suraj replies that he came late and, so, did not want to disturb him. After this, both become friends and sleep in the same room. Since both are lonely, they need company. But one day the narrator offends him by his joke. Suraj does not come to him. He waits for him uptill eleven at night. After that he goes to search him and finds him at last. The friendship is restored.

When Suraj is away selling his merchandise, the narrator satisfies his sexual desire by lying naked on the floor of the room. The cool floor soothes his heated body.

> At this hour of the day I lie naked on the stone floor of my room because the floor is the coolest place of all. As I am too listless to work or sleep, I study my navel, the hairs on my belly, the languid aspect of my genitals, and the hair on my legs and thighs....
>
> Of all the joys of the senses, I think it is the sense of touch I relish most—contact with the cool floor on a hot day. That is why I lie naked in my room so that all my flesh is in touch with cool stones.[6]

What the narrator speaks about himself is true with almost all adolescents when they are alone. The adolescents talk about their sex life and problems among them. Sometimes an adolescent is derided and at other times given a solution. Suraj and the narrator talk freely. Suraj tells him that he is afraid of women but has the desire to possess one. His friend tells Suraj that not every woman is made for every man and assures him that he will bring a girl for him, who will make him happy.

This is Kamla, the other version of Mrinalini in *Vagrants in the Valley,* very small, rather delicate, but more skilled in love-making than any of her colleagues. He further says that she is patient and particularly fond of young and inexperienced. Besides, she is only twenty three years old but has been in the profession for four years. After he goes on telling how he met Kamla and how he became her friend.

One thing is surprising that she has a husband. But, in fact, she is a prostitute in the house owned by Govind Ram. She says to the narrator:

> I have no family, silly man! I have a husband who is happy only if I can make myself attractive to others. He is skinny and smells of garlic and he has given my father five acres of land for the favour of having a wife half his age. But it is Seth Govind Ram who really owns me. My husband is only his servant.[7]

If we read the passage again, we can easily understand the plight of poor women in hill areas. As their parents cannot marry them off to suitable bridegrooms and are badly in need of money, they practically sell off their daughters to well-off middle-age men. The case of Kamla is worse. It is Seth Govind Ram who buys her for five acres and makes her a prostitute.

Bond is oblivious of this fact but his faithful narration reveals the ugly horrifying evil in the hill society. This practice of selling girls and employing them for prostitution is prevalent in the tribal societies of Madhya Pradesh also.

The theme of sex continues for a few more pages in the novel but in a superficial manner. A serious reader will feel that Bond's faculty has waned and in order to sustain the story of the novel he goes on adding episodes to bring it to its full length. Here is the bawdy scene, unreal and disquieting.

> Suraj was always a bit embarrassed with her. At first I thought it was because of my presence in the room. But when I offered to leave, he protested. He told me that he would have been completely helpless if I was not present all the time. In fact, I think he slept with Kamla only in order to please me.[8]

The same kind of episode about Ramu, Deep Chand's younger brother, is narrated.

> Once when he had his arm gashed by a knife in a street fight, he came to me for treatment.... He was very grateful and rewarded me with the story of his life. It was a chronicle of disappointed females, all of whom had been seduced by Ramu in fantastic circumstances and had been discarded by him after he had slept with each but once. Ramu boasted that he did not go twice to the same woman.

> All this was good-natured lying, as it was well-known that a girl-teaser like Ramu had never seen anything more than a well-shaped ankle. But apparently Ramu believed in many of his own adventures, which in his mind had acquired a legendary aspect.
>
> I did not ask him how he got his arm cut because I knew he would give me a fantastic explanation involving his honour and a lady's dishonour. Later, I discovered that an irate brother had stabbed him for spreading discreditable rumours about his sister.[9]

There are many adolescents who boast of their sexual adventures, partly true and largely false; and they do this just to impose their personality on their friends and acquaintances like the hero in J.M. Synge's *Playboy of the Western World.* What Bond fails to do is to show the tragedy of such boastful adolescents. If we read books on the psychology of adolescence, the experts advise teachers in schools and parents to watch the movement and behaviour of such young people and bring them to the right and normal path of life. Bond simply creates humour; it seems that he himself has not crossed the stage of adolescence in this novel.

The story of Ganpat also does not fit in well with the plot of the novel. First he tells the story of the agitation of beggars who are going to be taxed by the government. Then he describes Ganpat, leader of the beggars, who speaks good English. When he asks Ganpat why he is doubled up and if he gives the true explanation he will pay him four annas. Ganpat replies that he will tell the story behind his doubling up if he does not disclose the secret to other people. When assured, he narrates his past story.

He says that once he was a well-to-do farmer and had a beautiful wife. Life was happy but an incident changed the course of his life and made him a crippled beggar.

He owned several acres of land when he was young and newly married. He used to carry his produce on a bullock cart to the market which was five miles away and return at night when there was dark. He passed by a pipal tree every night. People said that it was a haunted tree but he did not believe them. The story was that Bippin, a young man, was looted by a gang of dacoits and hanged on that pipal tree. After becoming a ghost he took revenge on a person who looked like a dacoit. One night while he was going on his bullock cart Bippin jumped from the tree and caught hold of him because he looked like a dacoit. When he said that he was a poor man, not a dacoit, Bippin said that he would go his home and see whether he was speaking truth. Then he said to Ganpat,

> I have so arranged it...that no one but you will be able to see me. And another thing. I must sleep beside you every night, and no one must know of it. If you tell anyone about me, I'll kill you immediately.

So Bippin came to live with him, and he slept beside him every night and they got on very well together. He was as good as his word and money flowed into his house. But another trouble started. His wife began to suspect him. She and the members of her and his families insisted him on telling why he slept all alone. At last he told them the whole story. Bippin came to know that he had spoken everything. He did not come to his house and began to live in the tree. The next time when he was returning from the market, Bippin pounced upon him and accused him of betraying his friend. Ganpat tried to explain his position but Bippin would not listen. He, then, picked up a stout stick and struck him thrice on the back. He hit so hard that he bent up double.

This story as narrated by the beggar Ganpat is incredible. But such stories are quite common in villages. Nowadays, even a number of television channels are televising such stories. However, for a serious reader this story adds humour and what is more important is the theme of friendship and loneliness. The ghost feels lonely in the tree and so needs the company of Ganpat and punishes him because he has betrayed him.

After this digression comes the central point of the plot: the narrator's visit to Delhi. He asks Suraj if he should go to Delhi. Suraj encourages him to go there. Then he asks him to accompany him upto Delhi but Suraj replies that he is unable to go with him at present but will join him there after his examination. The narrator discusses the future plan but is diffident of the future perspectives. He says:

> There is nothing definite. But I know the chance will not come until I leave this place and make my chances. There are one or two editors who have asked me to look them up. They could give me some work. And if I find an honest publisher I might be encouraged to write an honest book.[10]

Suraj advises him to write the book even if he does not find a publisher. The author agrees and then they both decide to save money to meet the expenses to be incurred on the trip to Delhi.

After this, there is a detailed description of Pipalnagar in different seasons and the pleasures of two friends till the narrator goes to Delhi. Pitambar, a rikshaw-puller, takes him his home which is at a distance of five miles. The free atmosphere and the greenery around charm him and, so, he decides to come out of the town occasionally and enjoy the beauty of nature. One day, he hires a bicycle and both he and Suraj ride it and go out of the town. After sometime, Suraj gets down because sitting on the bar he finds that his legs are cramped. So, they walk on foot a distance of two miles, till they reach a tree which they never saw in their life. The trunk, the branches and even the leaves are crooked. There is a hole in the trunk and when they reach there, two parrots fly out of it and swoop into the nearby field. The whole scene is refreshing. They lie under the tree and take rest. Suraj sleeps but the narrator watches the rural scene with great pleasure. He describes it in a poetic language.

> I smelt the grass and the old bricks round the well and the promise of rain.
>
> I felt Suraj's fingers touching my arm and the sun creeping over my cheek.
>
> I opened my eyes and saw the clouds on the horizon and Suraj still asleep, his arm thrown across his eyes to keep away the glare.[11]

After sometime Suraj wakes. He says that it may rain. So they start for home. But before they reach Pipalnagar it starts raining heavily. They enjoy it and sing a song all the way. They reach the room, change their clothes and, after meal, go to sleep. Suraj as usual sleeps; besides he has fever, the reason being the rain. The narrator sleeps too but wakes in the middle of night when the beams of the full moon fall on his face. It is said that the full moon makes people dreamy and their imagination takes a soaring flight—"Poets, lovers and lunatics are all moon-struck." The narrator describes the activities and dreams of the people whom he knows well.

> People are restless tonight, with the moon shining through their windows. Suraj turns restlessly in his sleep, Kamla, having sent away a drunken customer, will be bathing herself as she always does before she finally sleeps.... Deep Chand is lying on his cot, dreaming of electric razors and a plush haircutting saloon in the capital, with the Prime Minister as his client. And Seth Govind Ram, unable to sleep because of the accusing moonlight, paces his veranda, worrying about his rent, counting up his assets, and wondering if he should stand for election to the Legistative Assembly.[12]

The narrator, too, has a dream—the dream of love and of becoming a successful original writer. In his real life Somi, Kishen and Mrs. Lal were best friends. Somi was the dearest of all. He writes in *Scenes*:

> To return to Somi, he was one of those friends I never saw again as an adult, so he remains transfixed in my memory as eternal youth, dream-bright, unchanging....
>
> I have often dreamt of Somi, and it is always the same dream.... We meet in a fairground, set up on the old parade ground. In the dream I am a man but he is still a boy. We wander through the fairground, enjoying all that it has to offer, in much the same way that we have enjoyed all that life had to offer.[13]

Suraj, in this novel, is a displacement of Somi. He is a lanky Punjabi and as tall as Somi and accompanies the narrator, obviously Rusty of the previous novels, when the latter goes to enjoy nature. The second half of *Delhi is Not Far* is mainly about Suraj and the narrator in Pipalnagar. First the change of seasons is described. The summer is the hottest season and it makes people restless.

> In June, the lizards hang listlessly on the walls, scanning their horizon in rain. Insects seldom show up—either the heat has killed them, or they are sleeping and breeding in cracks in the plaster. The lizards wait and wait....
>
> All Pipalnagar is waiting for its release from the oppressive heat of June.[14]

People wait eagerly for the arrival of the rainy season. At the end of June, clouds gather near the horizon. Soon they cover the sky and a cool breeze heralds the strong wind. Big drops platter on roofs at random. Then the heavy rain comes to quench the thirst of the earth. Bond is a keen observer of nature, children and teenagers. Here is a lively description.

> Rain upon Pipalnagar and until the rain stops, Pipalnagar is fresh and clean and alive. The children run out of their houses glorying in their nakedness. They are innocent and unashamed. Older children, by no means innocent, but by all means unashamed, romp through the town, inviting disapproval of their elders and, presumably, betters.[15]

The rain swirls over the trees and roofs of the town. The dry earth soaks it fast in the beginning but later on allows it to change into small streams running fast down on the slopes and making a broad stream. The earth exudes a fragrance that comes only in the first rains every year. The narrator battles against the elements. The wind pushes the door and he finds it difficult to shut it. The rain comes through the opening and drenches his cot. By the time he is able to shut the door he finds the roof leaking and water trickling down the walls. He places a tin and a mug at the places of seepage and leak and when he is satisfied that everything is under control, he sits on the cot and watches through the window the roof-tops of the houses before him.

Then he hears a loud banging on the door. It is Suraj. Impatient, he puts a pressure on the door which opens easily. He is fully soaked with water. He takes off his clothes and sits on the cot to dry himself up. After that the narrator talks about his ambition.

> One day I will write a book, I tell him. "Not a murder story but a real book, about real people. Perhaps it will be about you and me and Pipalnagar. And then we will break away from Pipalnagar, fly away life eagles, and our troubles will be over and fresh new troubles will begin. I do not mind difficulties, as long as they are new difficulties."[16]

It seems here that despite the love for Pipalnagar, he is ready to quit it for better prospects. He likes Deep Chand, Ramu, Pitambar, Kamla and Suraj and it will be painful for him to live without them but as Pipalnagar is not the right place for his creative activity, he must go to Delhi. Of course, he wants his people to be with him. This is why he asks Suraj to accompany him. Suraj's reply is practical.

"First I must pass my exams", said Suraj. "Without a certificate one can do nothing, go nowhere."

He tells Suraj that there is no conflict between them on the issue; he will write books and Suraj will study his course books. Suraj starts reading but he does not write; on the other hand he watches his beautiful face and the manner of reading.

An earthquake occurs for five seconds in Pipalnagar, the first earthquake in thirty years. A low, ominous rumble precedes it. People come out of the house. Suraj tumbles. When they come out, they find people in the street surrounding a seventy-year-old man who has jumped from the upper story of his house and broken his neck. Many people assemble in the temples and pray to God for their safety and welfare. In the meantime, it begins raining. But no one has the courage to go inside. In the meantime there is another tremor to confirm their fear. The narrator and Suraj do not want to be drenched in the rain, standing on the road. So they move on to the other side of the town. When they reach the outskirts, they find Pitambar dancing. They ask for the reason of dancing. The reply is funny.

"Why are you dancing on the road?" I asked.

"Because I am happy, that's why", said Pitambar.

"And what makes you so happy, my friend?"

"Because I am dancing on the road", he replied.[17]

The rest of the chapter describes the mooning of the two friends. They go to the riverside, gossip and bathe and swim there. They play in the open places in the forest and wrestle on the sandy bank of the river. Though the narrator is stouter and heavier than Suraj, it is Suraj who pins him down. Once they decide to go out of the town. They journey first by rail and then by bus. They reach the hills and enjoy the salubrious climate. For going there is the need of money. As they have no savings, the narrator pawns his gold ring for one hundred rupees. The money lasts for four days. The change of place has a healthy effect on Suraj. The bouts of epilepsy are reduced. Even the intensity is lessened. Earlier, there was the shadow of death in his eyes but now there is brightness and hope for life. He has grown stronger too. He studies along with Aziz seriously. The result comes out and he is successful. It gives both friends great joy.

From page 813 to the end, the novel relates the mixed fortune of the narrator. He is called to Delhi for an interview. As he has been living shabbily, he needs a shirt. The few he has are either torn at shoulders or frayed at the collars. He knows that most of the artists and creative writers are shabbily dressed but it is not the proper time, he feels, to display his poverty. The problem is a shirt, Suraj has an old red-striped T-shirt which he washes every second evening. But he cannot wear it because it is tight for Suraj even. What he needs is a white shirt. Deep Chand has shirts of bright colour and Pitambar is of no help. Finally, he goes to Kamla. She assures him and asks him to come next day. She gives him a shirt next morning and, also, a pair of silver cuff-links. It surprises him. Being asked she narrates how cleverly she got it from one of her customers.

> "One of my visitors", she replied with a shrug, "He was about your size. As he was quite drunk when he went home, he did not realize that I had kept his shirt. He had removed it to show me his muscles, as I kept telling him that he hadn't any to show."[18]

Once the arrangement for going to Delhi is finalised, he feels the sense of freedom. He says:

> Freedom.
>
> The moment the bus was out of Pipalnagar, and the fields opened out on all sides, I knew I was free; that I had always been free, held back by my own weakness, lacking the impulse and the imagination to break away from an existence that had become habitual for years.[19]

He is happy and so the whole world is happy. Sitting in the bus he thinks that the driver, the conductor, the passengers, the farmers in the fields and on their bullock carts are happy. He takes a small child on his knees and points out the camels, buffaloes, vultures and pariah dogs. Reaching Delhi, he goes to the editor of the Urdu weekly, who invited him to join the post of literary editor. He does not say anything about the salary and, so he also replies in a roundabout way. Returning to his place of stay he curses himself for not accepting the job in straightforward words. He writes a long letter to Suraj in which he describes everything that happened in Delhi on the first two days and the wanderings of his mind.

He is a changed man. He visits Chandni Chowk, the centre of trade and commerce, where business goes on all days.

> And if on a Sunday the shops must close, they merely spill out on the pavement and across the tram-lines—toys, silks and cottons, glassware, china, basket work, furniture, carpets and perfumes—it is as busy as on any market-day, and the competition louder and more fierce.[20]

He visits the important places of Delhi. At night time he hears the whistling of engines of trains going to different directions and like "a child conjures up visions of places with sweet names like Kumbekonam, Krishnagiri, Mahabalipuram and Polonnaruwa." He thinks of India, multi-people and multicultural.

> Ours is a land of many people, many races; their diversity gives it colour and character. For all Indians to be alike would be as dull as for all sexes to be the same, or for all humans to be normal. In Delhi, too, there is a richness of

> race, though the Punjabi predominates—in shops, taxis, motor workshops and carpenters' sheds. But in the old city there are still many Muslims following traditional trades—butchers, painters, makers of toys and kites. South Indians have filled our offices; Rajasthanis move dexterously along the scaffolding of new buildings springing up everywhere; and in the surrounding countryside nomadic Gujjars still graze their cattle, while settled villagers find their lands selected for trails of new tubewells, pumps, fertilizers and ploughs.[21]

He describes Delhi as it was in the early fifties—expanding and getting busier everyday, a sharp contrast to Pipalnagar, a small town in the north where life is still slow and peaceful.

He returns to Pipalnagar after getting the job. The salary of three hundred rupees is more than enough for a single man like him. He had the feeling of freedom when he left Pipalnagar for Delhi. But after returning home his mind changes; he cannot break the bond of love that binds him to the town and the people.

Suraj waits for the narrator on the platform. When the express train arrives at the station, both friends meet but they speak little. It is only after taking tea that the narrator breaks the silence in the room. He speaks his mind to Suraj.

> "It is three hundred a month", I said, "but we should be able to manage on that, if we are careful. And now that you have done matriculation, you will be able to join the polytechnic. So we will both be busy. And when we are not working, we shall have all Delhi to explore. It will be better in the city. One should live either in a city or in a village. In a village everyone knows you intimately. In a city no one has the slightest interest in you. But in a town like Pipalnagar everyone knows you, nobody loves you. When you die, you are forgotten; while you live, you are only a subject for malicious conversation. Poor Pipalnagar.... Will you be sorry to leave the place, Suraj?"[22]

The change in his attitude surprises Suraj. He emphatically says: "Yes I will be sorry. This is where I have lived." It is clear that Suraj can leave his friend but not Pipalnagar as he is deeply rooted in its soil.

But the narrator has a different view.

> This is where I've existed. I only began to live when I realized I could leave the place.

He makes a distinction between "exist" and "live" and by "live" he means existing purposefully and meaningfully. Uptill now he has lived like an illiterate or ignorant person; his life will be meaningful in Delhi only. But the replies of Suraj begin to change his mind again. He realizes that there are people in Pipalnagar who love him.

Deep Chand is happy to know that Suraj and he are leaving for Delhi. He says that he, too, can make money by cutting hair in Delhi because even girls are going to have short hair. He shall keep a special saloon for ladies which Ramu can attend. The reason for making Ramu the keeper of the ladies' saloon is that women feel safe with him. At his words Ramu winks at the narrator in the mirror. Ramu, in fact, is a big eve-teaser. Deep Chand goes on cutting his hair and the rhythmic sound of his scissors make the narrator sleep. Deep Chand does not charge anything as it is the last hair cut and shave.

The next friend is Kamla. Her house is at a distance of five miles from Pipalnagar. He goes to her village and waits behind some trees on the outskirts of the village until he sees her playing with a little boy. He whistles to her. When she hears the sound, she looks at him and she makes sign to wait for her. He stands among the sal trees. She comes to him but is a little far. He follows her doorsteps and then sees her near a stream. A romantic place indeed. They sit together, gossip together and finally he asks her to go with him to Delhi where he can support her. He kisses her out of love. But when he asks her to come away from Pipalnagar, she politely refuses and explains the reason.

> Because you do not really want me to. For you a woman would only be a liability. You are free like birds, you and Suraj, you can go where you like and do as you like. I cannot help you in any way. And what use is a woman to a

> man if she cannot help him? I have helped you pass your time in Pipalnagar. That is something. I am part of this place. Neither Pipalnagar nor I can change. But you can, simply by going away.[23]

When he asks her if she would come when he starts making a living in Delhi, her reply is that things are not that simple and finally that she has a husband. It is only after his and Govind Ram's death she will be free to do anything. He feels frustrated at her reply. Then she says that it is Suraj who has stolen his heart, not she and after this she runs towards her home with a final wave.

Suraj and he go to the bus stand in the morning next day to catch the bus to Delhi. He looks at the town, beautifully ensconced in the lap of nature.

> A land of thrusting hills. Terraced hills, wood-covered and windswept. Mountains where the gods speak gently to the lonely heart. Hills of green and grey rock, misty at dawn, hazy at noon, molten at sunset; where fierce fresh torrents rush to the valley below.
>
> A quiet land of fields and ponds, shaded by ancient trees and ringed with palms, where sacred rivers are touched by temples; where temples are touched by the southern seas.[24]

This passage, of course, describes Pipalnagar but when we read the second paragraph the clause "where temples are touched by the southern seas", we begin to think of Kanyakumari and Rameshwaram and enlarge the meaning of Pipalnagar that the author means it India. Ruskin Bond's love of India is manifest in this paragraph.

The paragraph that follows it reveals his love of Pipalnagar and its people and also, if we connect it with the previous paragraph, to India and her people.

The last two concluding paragraphs are his resolve to write about Pipalnagar and its people.

> This is the real land, the land I should write about. My mohalla is but a sickness, a wasting disease, and I should turn aside from it to sing instead of the splendours of tomorrow. But only yesterdays are splendid.... There are

other singers, sweeter than I, to sing of tomorrow. I can only sing of today of Pipalnagar, where I have lived and loved.

Yesterday I was sad and tomorrow I may be sad again, but today I know that I am happy. I want to live on and on, delighting like a pagan in all that is physical; and I know that one lifetime, however long, cannot satisfy my heart.[25]

The last clause of the first paragraph of the quoted passage has the verbs "lived" and "loved". These words indicate the shift in the attitude of the speaker. Earlier while discussing with Suraj the future plan of living in Delhi he said that he *existed* in Pipalnagar and began to *live* after leaving it. The second contention was that no one loved in a small town like Pipalnagar. But now he is a changed man: he has lived in Pipalnagar and loved it and its people.

The novel as we see it is about a young writer's struggle for success. The title is already explained that it is an adaptation of Hazrat Nizamuddin's words to Tuglaque Shah: Delhi is still far. For an adolescent or post-adolescent the word "impossible" does not exist. The circumstances may be adverse or straining, he is never deterred. Besides, he has a zest for life. This is what happens with the narrator. He is a young man of twenty-five, a post-adolescent. A poor young man without any connection, he struggles for life. It is difficult for him to pay his rents. His scanty income is the money the editors of magazines send him as remuneration for his stories and detective novels. Advised by a Meerut publisher, he decides to write an original novel, a novel rooted in the earth where he lives.

Indirectly, this novel is his original work. Although he resolves to write about Pipalnagar, he, in fact, has already written the novel. Here he can be compared with W.B. Yeats, Yeats sees a fisherman. The fisherman is an Irishman who, in his opinion represents his people. After seeing him, he decides to write a poem:

Before I am old

I shall have written him one

Poem may be as cold

And passionate as the dawn.[26]

Though he says that he will write a poem in future, he, in reality, has already written it.

The novel is about Pipalnagar and its people—Suraj, Kamla, Deep Chand, Ramu, Seth Govind Ram and Aziz and other people. These people, barring the Seth, are all common people. Suraj is a student of matriculation and earns his living by selling combs and buttons. He is epileptic and, so, needs support. He is well-supported by the dreamy narrator and in turn supports him by his practicality. Kamla, although married to a person of insignificance, is a prostitute in the *chakla* (whore-house) owned by Seth Govind Ram. She loves the narrator and satisfies his sex whenever he needs and on his advice sleeps with Suraj too. Deep Chand is a barber who has a saloon. He supports his family with a low income. And there is his mischievous younger brother Ramu, the eve-teaser. Then we see Pitambar, a rikshaw-puller, who has a well-built body and who is always happy.

Pipalnagar is described in all seasons—summer, rain, autumn and winter. Ruskin Bond is a keen observer of nature. His mooning with Suraj in the fields and forests of Pipalnagar are romantic and charming. Since the rainy season is the most spectacular season in India and people wait eagerly for its arrival, it has been described in detail with great enthusiasm. Ruskin Bond writes in his reminiscence *Rain in the Mountains*:

> Each drop represents a little bit of creation—and of life itself. When the monsoon brings to northern India the first rains of summer, the parched earth opens its pores and quenches its thirst with a hiss of ecstasy. After baking in the sun for the last few months, the land looks cracked, dusty and tired. Now, almost over-night, new grass springs up, there is renewal everywhere, and the damp earth releases a fragrance sweeter than any devised by man.[27]

However, the author has not done justice to the seriousness of the theme. The narrator's struggle for becoming a good original writer is not depicted in detail nor the love and mutual co-operation of the common people. It begins in realism and ends in realism but the middle, in spite of its poetic language, is far away from the stark realities of life. We have only an idyllic picture of Pipalnagar.

NOTES

1. *Ruskin Bond: Collected Fiction*, 765.
2. *Ibid.*, 765.
3. *Ibid.*, 766.
4. *Ibid.*, 773.
5. *Ibid.*, 779-80.
6. *Ibid.*, 777.
7. *Ibid.*, 781.
8. *Ibid.*, 782-83.
9. *Ibid.*, 787.
10. *Ibid.*, 786.
11. *Ibid.*, 792.
12. *Ibid.*, 793.
13. *Scenes from a Writer's Life*, 162-63.
14. *Ruskin Bond: Collected Fiction*, 794.
15. *Ibid.*, 798.
16. *Ibid.*, 799.
17. *Ibid.*, 801.
18. *Ibid.*, 813.
19. *Ibid.*
20. *Ibid.*, 816.
21. *Ibid.*, 817.
22. *Ibid.*, 818.
23. *Ibid.*, 821.
24. *Ibid.*, 822.
25. *Idem.*, 822.
26. W.B. Yeats, "The Fisherman", *Collected Poems* (London: Macmillan, 1950), 167.
27. Ruskin Bond, *Rain in the Mountains* (New Delhi: Penguin, 1993), 105.

5

A Flight of Pigeons

A Flight of Pigeons has its source in the annuls of Indian history. What the British people called Mutiny was our First War of Independence. All the events in the novel are related to the 1857 War of Independence. What is special in the novel is that the author is not concerned with the big personalities like Bahadur Shah Jafar, Nana Sahab, Tatya Tope, Lakshmi Bai, Kunwar Singh and other fighters of freedom nor the British generals. He is concerned with a middle class British family and the middle class Indian families who, in spite of the bitter war, retain their humanity.

He writes in the "Notes" to the novel that he heard the story from his father:

> I first heard the story of Mariam and her daughter from my father, who was born in the Shahjahanpur military cantonment a few years after the Mutiny. That, and my interest in the accounts of those who had survived the 1857 uprising, took me to Shahjahanpur on a brief visit in the late 1960s. It was one of those small UP towns that had resisted change, and there were no high-rise buildings or blocks of flats to stifle the atmosphere. I found the old church of St. Mary's without any difficulty, and beside it a memorial to those who were killed there on that fateful day. It was surrounded by a large, open parade ground, bordered by mango groves and a few old bungalows. It couldn't have been very different in Ruth Labadoor's time.

> The little river Khannaut was still crossed by a bridge of boats.[1]

Just on the top of the same page where the quoted passage occurs, Bond quotes two lines from *The Meerut Mofussilite,* 1858.

> Mr. Lemaistre, a clerk in the Collector's office, was killed in the church, and the fate of his daughter is unknown.

The novel begins with a prologue which reads like a page from history but once we enter into the main body of the novel we find that it is a world seen through the eyes of the adolescent girl Ruth. We can say that it is a novel written by an adolescent. Secondly, the prologue is actual history but after that what happens in the novel is the product of the author's imagination stirred by the story he heard from his father. Mr. Lemaistre becomes Mr. Labadoor.

We learn in the prologue the events in 1857 in Shahjahanpur. The opening paragraphs briefly summarise the beginning of India's First War of Independence. For the reasons best known to Ruskin Bond, he uses the words "revolt" and "mutinous regiments", whereas Marx and Engels called it War of Independence.* He does not mention the name of Mangal Pandey, the first person to shoot the English officers.

> The revolt broke out at Meerut on the 10th of May, at the beginning of a very hot and oppressive summer. The sepoys shot down their English officers; there was rioting and looting in the city; the jail was broken open, and armed convicts descended on English families living in the city and cantonment, setting fire to houses and killing the inmates. Several mutinous regiments marched to Delhi, their principal rallying-point, where the peaceable, poetry-loving Emperor Bahadur Shah suddenly found himself the figurehead of revolt.
>
> The British army which had been cooling off in Shimla, began its long march to Delhi. But meanwhile, the conflict had spread to other cities. And on the 30th of May there

---

* Marx and Engels considered it the war of independence whereas the Britishers called it a mutiny. Vide their book *The First Indian War of Independence* 1857-1858, (Moscow: Progress Publishers, 1959).

> was much excitement in the magistrate's office at Shahjahanpur some 250 miles east of Delhi.[2]

After this he shifts the focus to the small town of Shahjahanpur and its Anglo-Indian and British officers. The first event is the burning of Redman's bungalow by Javed Khan, a local tough. He is arrested but is released because of the lack of evidence. The burning of Redman's bungalow does not alert the Collector of Shahjahanpur nor the other officers. A party is arranged in the house of Dr. Bowling and the entire British community enjoys it. The only person absent is Mr. Labadoor who has married Mariam, a Muslim and French hybrid, and whose daughter is Ruth, the principal character in the novel. Mr. Labadoor is forty-two, Mariam thirty-eight and Ruth thirteen still reading in a school at Fatehgarh but removed a fortnight before, because her mother feels, she will be safer at home.

The great quality of Mariam is that she mixes well with the Indian people, makes social calls and gossips with servants. She hears from them the news of Meerut and the words of a *fakir* that the days of East India company are numbered. Sensing the coming danger, she asks her husband to avoid the party in the house of Bowling and also the church prayer on next Sunday.

Mr. Labadoor does not attend the party but goes to the church. From here, the author withdraws from the scene and lets "Ruth take up the story", Once Ruth starts telling story, we feel we are in a world as seen by an adolescent. The story is a series of episodes and we feel that Ruth's journey is a kind of Odyssey.

She goes to the church with her father. She is scared when a few sepoys, going for their morning bath to the river, stare fiercely at them and she clings to her father for protection. Her father does not find anything unusual and they both go to the church. They begin their prayer but while they are in the middle of it, they are attacked by miscreants.

> Their faces were covered up to their noses, and they wore tight loincloths as though they had prepared for a wrestling bout; but they held naked swords in their hands.[3]

She escapes but her father is heavily injured. After the departure of the assailants, she goes to her father who is bleeding profusely and bandages his face with the handkerchief which is in his pocket. But one handkerchief is insufficient. So she uses her own handkerchief also and bandages his face. When she has done so, he wishes to go home but he is too weak to walk. There he advises her to take him to the church. After reaching the church she observes the tragic scene—armless Englishmen attacked by fierce sepoys. Almost all the people in the church are badly injured. She wants to be with her wounded father but has to run home to bring a *dolie* to carry him. The road to her home is calm and quiet; no one says anything to her but when she reaches home, she finds it in flames.

Stunned she stands there. In the meantime, a Hindu Kayastha Lala Ramjimal meets her and tells her that her family is safe and then he takes her his home. Her mother leaves a sigh of relief when she sees her. Ruth then, tells the incident at the church. Ramjimal goes to the church where Mr. Labadoor, Ruth's father, is dying. He sees Ramjimal, recognizes him and then dies. Ramjimal reports his death in a few simple words.

Ruth and her mother Mariam are destitutes, like two birds in a desert. But Ramjimal's humanity saves their lives. He brings them to his house and hides them so that the miscreants would not know who they are. His humanity is manifest in the following words of Ruth:

> His motives were always personal and if he helped us, it was not because we belonged to the ruling class—my father was probably the most junior officer in Shahjahanpur—but because he had known us for many years, and had grown fond of my mother, who had always treated him as a friend and equal.[4]

Although his own family is big,—Mrs. Ramjimal, mother-aunt and sister,—he does not hesitate to accommodate Ruth, Mariam, Ruth's grandmother, Anet, her mother's half-brother, Pillo, and his mother. Besides, there are the maid-servants Champa and Lado and the two spaniels, one white and the other black. In short, there are eight people in Lala's house.

They are given food but they do not feel the desire to eat and Mariam is unable to check her tears after knowing her husband's death. We must admire Lala Ramjimal's strength and patience to bear the burden of twelve females single-handed in those difficult days.

Ruth and her family are given meal only once in twenty-four hours but they are happy with that big meal. The house is an ordinary mud building, a typical Indian house. On the second day of their arrival, Ruth overhears Ramjimal's mother speaking to him:

> Lalaji, you have made a great mistake in bringing these *Angrezans* into our house. What will people say? As soon as the rebels hear of it, they will come and kill us.[5]

Then there is Lala's reply:

> I have done what is right. I have not given shelter to *Angrezans*. I have given shelter to friends. Let people say or think as they please.

He keeps a vigil on his house and chains the front door. His humanity and hospitality is as great as that of the legendary Hatim Tai of Arabia.

Ruth writes:

> He seldom went out of the house, and was usually to be seen seated before the front door, either smoking his small hookah, or playing chess with some friend who happened to drop by. After a few days people began to suspect that there was somebody in the house about whom Lala was being very discreet....
>
> It is a wonder that we were able to live undiscovered for as long as we did....[6]

Ruth and Mariam and other members of the family stay in Lala Ramjimal's house for two weeks. At that time people ask him the reason for sitting in the verandah all the time. His reply is that after the departure of the foreigners, his business has come to a halt and since he has nothing to do, he sits idle. They suggest him to meet the Nawab.

It so happens that after destroying the British government's buildings and officers, the freedom fighters establish their own government. The leader of the soldiers appoints Qadar Ali Khan as the Nawab, Nizam Ali, a pensioner is made Kotwal and responsible posts are given to Javed Khan and Nizam Ali Khan but the latter refuses the post.

Later on, Lala Ramjimal describes the burial of the British officers. He says that a few labourers and he managed to dig trenches and lay the dead bodies of captain James, Dr. Bowling, Father MacCullum, Mr. Smith and Mariam's husband, Mr. Labadoor in the church yard. Though the whole description is painful for the women, especially Mariam, they get a sigh of relief that their man was buried according to Christian rites.

Fearing that they may be caught and killed they change their names and assume Muslim names as they are all well-versed in Urdu and Ruth's grandmother comes from a good Muslim family of Rampur. Ruth is called Khurshid, her cousin Anet being short of stature, Nanni, Pillo is given the name Ghulam Hussain, and his mother becomes known as Ghulam Hussain's mother. Grandmother (Granny) is Bari-bi and since Ruth's mother has already the Muslim name Mariam, there is no need to change her name.

They live happily there but Mariam, Ruth's mother, is always apprehensive. She sleeps in daytime but remains awake the whole night. Besides, she asks for a knife. When Lala Ramjimal gives her an old rusty Knife, she cleans it and sharpens it with great labour. Other members of the family do not sense any impending danger but she does. Her premonition proves true one night.

Ruth narrates:

> It was ten o'clock and everyone had gone to bed, except Mother, who still sat at the foot of my cot. I was just dozing off when she remarked that she could smell jasmine flowers, which was strange, because there was no jasmine bush near the house. At the same time a clod of earth fell from the high wall, and looking up we saw in the dark the figure of a man stretched across it. There was another man

a little further along, concealed in the shadows of a neem tree that grew at the end of the yard. Mother drew her knife from beneath her pillow, and called out that she would pierce the heart of the first man who attempted to lay hands on us. Impressed by her ferocity, which was like that of a tigress guarding her young, the intruders quietly disappeared into the night.[7]

Here, we see Mariam in full glory. Though her husband is killed and she is hiding with all the members of the family in the house of an Indian, she has not lost her courage and fortitude. She is brave enough to challenge the miscreants and save the family from tragedy. The other incident, while they are in Lala's house, is more alarming for them but it also reveals to us the humanity and endurance of the maid-servant Lado.

It so happens that Lado, one of the two servants who followed Ruth's family, living with them in Lala's family, is searched by her daughter after the outbreak. She has a daughter married to a local sword-cleaner. This sword-cleaner comes to know that Lado is with the *Firangis* in Lala's house. So he comes to Lalaji on 23 June and asks him about his mother-in-law and threatens him if he does not allow her to come out of his house he will face dire consequences. He also wants to enter into his house and search her. Lala's reply is stern: he will never allow anyone to enter the ladies' apartment in his house.

Lado comes to know everything. She expresses the desire to leave the house. She touches their feet and says that she does not want to bring trouble to them. Everybody is touched by her loyalty. When she reaches home, she is brought to the court of Nawab Qadar Ali. The Nawab asks her about Ruth's family. She says that they died in the fire and Mariam (she calls her Labadoor-Mem) jumped into the Khannaut, the river that flows by the town. But the Nawab disbelieves her and threatens her. But the frail woman remains firm. She swears that she has no idea if they are alive. At last the Nawab asks two swordsmen to catch hold of her by hair and run the sword through her throat. Even though the sword touches her throat she says that they are dead. The Nawab releases her as innocent.

"Well, since you are not afraid even of the sword, I suppose you know nothing. Let her go"[8]

Suddenly, there is a change in the administration of Shahjahanpur. Nawab Qadar Ali is replaced by Nawab Ghulam Qadar Khan, a strict person but considerate to children and women. He is of the opinion that the male foreigners are wicked and, so, they should be killed but women and children, being innocent, should be spared. Mariam and Granny are happy but their happiness is short-lived. Lala Ramjimal has exhausted all his money and is, as there is no business, unable to support the family. He, therefore, proposes to go to Bareilly where his brother lives. All agree and they decide to start their journey in two carts. But their misfortune comes earlier.

About thirty persons under the leadership of Javed Khan, the greatest dare-devil of the town, knock at the door of Ramjimal and ask for the foreigners. Mrs. Ramjimal comes to the door and tells that there is none but they unheed her words and break open the door of the room where Ruth and Mariam are hiding. Mariam is fierce and her bloodshot eyes calm Javed Khan but he recognizes Ruth and catches hold of her hand. Ruth is terrified. Mariam accompanies her. They all walk in the summer heat bare-foot and bare-head. They have blisters in their feet. At last, they reach a tamarind tree where they take rest. There a *pir* instructs Javed not to harm the ladies in any way. Javed promises to act upon his advice. Soon they come to Javed's house where her aunt, called Kothiwali, and his wife, Qabil are presently living. Mariam introduces herself and tells her ancestry that she comes from Rampur and her daughter as Khurshid and that she married an Englishman who was killed at the church and, now, she is a widow.

Javed promises to his aunt that he will not harm them. All that he wants is to marry Khurshid (Ruth) whom he loves deeply. His words shock Qabil but she is helpless as he has every right to have another wife according to law.

When we read this episode, two facts come clearly before us. The first is that there was little communal divide between the Hindus and the Muslims. Javed and his people say nothing to Ramjimal and his family for giving shelter to the *firangis*. Secondly, they have no desire to harm the innocent and defenceless women and children of the foreigners. Besides, Javed, a kind of hooligan, follows certain principles; he does not take Ruth by force. Finally, the common Indians are rather unconcerned about the British rule and even if they are, they do not bear enmity towards those foreigners whom they know personally. This is why Ruth and Mariam live honourably there and are neither harassed nor Ruth is molested.

Mariam and Ruth live there happily but one thing torments them and that is the absence of Granny, Anet, Pillo and his mother. Champa, the maid-servant, they think, is safe in the house of Ramjimal. They express their restlessness to Javed who promises that he will bring them safe. Javed is docile and obedient to Mariam only for the reason that he loves Ruth, now Khurshid to him. One day Ramjimal comes to Javed's house and reproaches him for forcibly taking the fugitives from his house. He says that Javed entered his house in his absence and had he been there in the house, Javed would enter it only over his dead body. Javed politely replies that he did not want to see him dead. Ramjimal returns the box of jewellery and the thirty rupees he received for selling the piece of gold. Mariam trusts his honesty so much that she does not feel the need to open the box and see its contents.

Soon Granny, Anet and Champa join them but not Pilloo and his mother. It so happens that after Javed's raid of the house is the intrusion of Mangal Khan, rough but generous. He takes Pilloo and his mother with him. Since Pillo is a boy of fourteen he is spared. Later on, Mangal Khan adopts him as his son.

Mariam and Ruth are invited by Kothiwali. They go there and live comfortably and happily. The War of Independence continues but now the freedom fighters are losing the battle. Delhi is recaptured by the British army and, slowly, the other towns. Now, Javed, Nawab, Mangal Khan and other freedom fighters have to save their own lives. Mariam, Ruth and other members of the family move to Shahjahanpur where they meet the Redmans family. After a long odyssey, they arrive home safe.

Although the novel has the 1857 war as its backdrop, it is more or less a family novel in the tradition of Jane Austen. The beginning gives us an ideal of what happened in a small town like Shahjahanpur when the freedom fighters attacked the British civilians. We feel sympathy for the slain people, especially Mr. Labadoor and Father MacCullam and also the burning of Mr. Labadoor's bungalow. We pity the fate of Mariam, Ruth, Granny, Anet, Pilloo and his mother because they are all innocent and have mixed with the Indian people.

They become a kind of refugee in the house of Lala Ramjimal, a Kayastha by birth but a businessman by profession, and since they cannot come out of the house, they live a really miserable life. Besides, they live in terror. There is the constant fear of being recognized and killed. Mariam, therefore, always keeps a knife and one night she threatens the intruders with it when they try to enter stealthily into the house.

They can resist such minor skirmishes but not the massive onslaught of Javed Khan. The worst happens; once the pride of the town they beg for mercy and, though their life is spared, Mariam and Ruth have to walk in the heat of the sun bare-foot and bare-head. But once they enter Javed's house, the perils of attacks by miscreants recede into oblivion. His wife Qabil, though she does not like Javed's proposal to marry Khurshid (Ruth), is civil to both mother and daughter. Qabil is happy that Mariam refuses the proposal by delaying tactics. Kothiwali, Javed's aunt (chachi), likes both Mariam and Khurshid (Ruth) and extends every kind of hospitality.

At the time of departure from Javed's house, she invites both of them. When they go there, she treats them well and they stay there for three months. She is the mother of two sons and one daughter. The entire family consists of her daughter, two sons, one daughter-in-law, one son-in-law and a number of grand children. Ruth describes her:

> Kothiwali was the widow of a landed proprietor in the District, and must have been about forty years old when

we knew her. She was tall, with black hair and eyes, a large mouth, small teeth coloured black with *missi** and paan. She wore no trinkets except for a round silver bangle on each hand, and a plain silver ring on her right small finger. Her face was always cheerful, and she possessed great spirit. She commanded great respect from the rest of her community, who often came to consult her when in difficulty.[9]

But the tenure of happiness is broken when Javed sends a message for their return. Javed is the most important male character in the novel. A young man of strong physique and ebullient temperament, he is both polite and arrogant at the same time. He follows the principles of Islam in his own way or the way he has been taught. Born in a well-to-do family, he forms a gang of his own to uproot the foreigners from the Indian soil. However, he is not like Nana Sahab, Tatya Tope, Binda Tiwari or Mangal Pandey. He is a simple man and is least interested in national politics; all that he strives for is the recovery of the lost glory of the Nawab of Shahjahanpur. Lala Ramjimal describes his activities:

> Javed Khan, as you know, is one of the biggest ruffians in the city. When the sepoys had returned to their lines after proclaiming the Nawab, Javed Khan paid a visit to their commander. On learning that the regiment was preparing to leave Shahjahanpur and join the Bareilly brigade, he persuaded the Subedar-Major, Ghansham Singh, to make a raid on the Rosa Rum Factory before leaving. A detachment, under Subedar Zorawar Singh, accompanied Javed Khan, and they took the road which passes by Jhunna Lal, the treasurer's house. There they halted and demanded a contribution from Jhunna Lal. It so happened that he had only that morning received a sum of six thousand rupees from the Tehsildar of Jalalabad, and this the Subedar seized at once.[10]

As Javed did not get anything, he set the factory on fire and "no less than 70000 gallons of rum, together with a

---

* A kind of powder black in colour to strengthen the gum and brighten teeth of Muslim women.

> large quantity of loaf sugar were destroyed. The rest was carried away. Javed Khan's share of loaf sugar was an entire cartload![11]

He goes to Lala Ramjimal with the intention to have Ruth whom he had seen before the revolt. He wants to marry her and, so, spares the lives of the people hiding there:

> Where is Labadoor's daughter? He demanded of Mother, gripping her by arm and looking intently into her face. 'No this is not her,' he said, dropping her hand and turning to look at me.
>
> 'This is the girl!' he exclaimed, taking me by the hand and dragging me away from Mother into the light of the courtyard.[12]

As said earlier, he is a simple-hearted and in spite of his cruelty, follows the principles of Islam and remains true to his word. When he, with his gang, rests under a tamarind tree, a pir happens to pass that way. Seeing the distressed women, the pir advises him to refrain from doing any harm to them:

> Javed, you have taken away the unfortunate to amuse yourself. Give me your word of honour that you will not ill-treat or kill them.[13]

At this Javed brings his sword to a slant before his face and says:

> I swear by my sword that I will neither kill nor ill-treat them.

Javed is never cruel to Ruth and her mother. This is evident in his own house; both mother and daughter are given full hospitality. When his proposal is politely declined, he says only this:

> 'I am in no hurry,' said Javed Khan. 'A matter of such importance cannot be settled in a day. Take a week, good woman. And do not forget that this is no sudden infatuation on my part. The girl has been in my mind for months. I am not Javed if I let the opportunity pass me by. Be easy in your mind—there is no hurry....'[14]

This is something surprising. Nobody would expect this kind of behaviour from Javed Khan, the greatest ruffian in Shahjahanpur. We can easily know the kind of man he is from these words to his wife.

"Don't be such a fool, Qabil!"

In fact, he has no feeling for his wife; she is his wife, a child producing machine, may be. Later on, he says in anger:

> "What did you say Qabil?" He asked sharply. "No, don't repeat it again. The demon is only slumbering in my breast, and it will take little to rouse it."[15]

He considers it to be his right to marry another woman even when his wife is alive or undivorced because the Muslim law permits it. His words terrify Ruth and anger his wife Qabil:

> I was full of resentment, but could say nothing and do nothing, except press closer to my mother and look at Javed Khan with all the scorn I could muster. Khan-Begum, too, must have been seeing this with indignation; but she too was helpless, because Javed was well within his rights to think in terms of a second wife.[16]

He gives a scorching look at Ruth. Ruth is fascinated like a rabbit before a python or large snake and is so terrified that she cannot take her eyes away from his gaze. She says "I was like a doomed bird, fascinated by the gaze of a rattlesnake." Here it is her mother who saves her. Mariam stares at him as though "she would plumb his dark soul to its innermost depths, and he quailed under her stern gaze." Javed defends himself:

> "Don't put me down for a common murderer", he said apologetically. "If I have taken lives, they have been those of infidels, enemies of my people. I am deserving of praise rather than blame."[17]

It is clear that he is good to Mariam and bears her words and fierce eyes only for the reason that he wants to marry Ruth. He is a blatant ruffian and his goodness is confined to his own people so long they obey him.

But it is difficult to blame him for his views and behavioural pattern. He is doing what his ancestors have done.

His words to Ruth's mother throw light on his way of thinking and doing. When Mariam says that he cannot marry a Christian, he protests loudly and asserts his position by quoting the examples of his father and uncle:

> "There is no reason why I may not", replied Javed Khan. "We Pathans can take a wife from any race or creed we please. And—" pausing as his wife let fall a petulant 'oh'! "I dare my wife to object to such a proceeding on my part. Did not my father take in a low-caste woman for her large, pretty eyes, the issue of that union being the brat, Safiullah—a plague on him!—and Kothiwali, whom you see here, was a low-caste Hindu who charmed my uncle out of his wits. So what harm can these be if I take a Christian for a wife?"[18]

He would have succeeded in his attempt if there were no opposition from his chachi Kothiwali, his wife Qabil and Ruth's mother Mariam. However he makes the proposal again. When Mariam takes some pretext, he very frankly says:

> I am an impatient man, Mariam, and life is not so long that I can wait an eternity to quench my desires. I have restrained myself out of respect for your wishes, and out of respect for you. But my desire to call your girl my wife grows stronger daily, and I am prepared to take any risk to have her for my own.[19]

Mariam's dilatory tactics pays her dividends. Javed is angry but he cannot do anything. In the meantime, the British army recovers and wins Delhi and other places. Javed is in trouble. He leaves Shahjahanpur. Ruth speaks about him:

> We heard that Kothiwali and Qamran and their families eventually returned to Shahjahanpur, after life had returned to normal. But Javed Khan disappeared and was never seen again. Perhaps, he had escaped into Nepal. It is more probable that he was caught and hanged with some other rebels.[20]

What can we say of Javed Khan? What kind of man is he? He is a young man bound by the traditions of his community. He considers it his duty to drive away the foreigners from the land of India. If he wanted, he could have married Ruth by force but he does not do so. It follows then that he lives by Islamic principles. He is not even harsh to them because he has made the promise before the saint, (pir). His argument that he can marry a Christian girl is validated by the convention he quotes. The sugar loaf he plunders at Rosa Rum Factory is used for making sherbat in Moharram; he does not sell it nor does he use it at home. He does not allow Sarfaraj to assault Ruth and Mariam and exchanges hot words on the issue.

Perhaps, it is his nobility, faithfulness and integrity that even the terrorised Ruth makes the following comments:

> Secretly, I have always hoped that he succeeded in escaping. Looking back on those months when we were his prisoners, I cannot help feeling a sneaking admiration for him. He was very wild and muddle-headed, and often cruel, but he was also very handsome and gallant, and there was in him a streak of nobility which he did his best to conceal. But perhaps, I really admire him because he thought I was beautiful.[21]

We shall agree with every word of her except the word "prisoner"; Javed always considered Ruth's mother his relative and Ruth, his future wife.

The most impressive character in the novel is Mariam, Ruth's mother. She is a Eurasian, her mother being a Muslim of Rampur and father a European. She is bold and beautiful and possesses the wonderful quality of forbearance. Made widow at a young age in the turbulent days of 1857, she has to support her daughter, her mother-in-law, Pillo and his mother, Anet and her mother two maid-servants and two dogs. Another woman in her situation would have broken but she musters courage and supports all the people dependent on her. When she comes to know about her husband's death, her reaction is quite natural.

> Hearing that we had both been killed, Mother's first impulse was to throw herself into the nearest well.[22]

But she recovers herself after Granny's request and realizes the truth that the whole family will die if she does not support them. Falling down from plenty to poverty, she adjusts herself with the family of Ramjimal and is ready to have one-time meal. There, she is always alert and once she drives away the two spies who come at night to find if there are foreigners in the house. She is bold enough to flash the knife she has borrowed from Ramjimal.

She shows the same kind of boldness before the muscular Javed. Javed Khan enters Ramjimal's house, goes to Ruth and Mariam, recognizes the former and then holds her hand firmly. When he starts taking her with him, Mariam first begs for his mercy and then looks sternly at him.

> "No!" cried my mother in a tone of anguish, throwing herself in front of me. "If you would take my daughter's life, take mine before hers. I beg of you by the sword of Ali!"
>
> Her eyes were bloodshot, starting out of their sockets, and she presented a magnificient, and quite terrifying sight. I think she frightened me even more than the man with the raised sword; but I slung to her instinctively, and tried to wrest my arm from the man's grasp. But so impressed was he by Mother's display that he dropped the point of sword and in a gruff voice commanded us both to follow him quietly if we valued our lives.[23]

She is equally sociable and tactful. She moves out of her house before it is set on fire only because she got the information earlier.

> While most of the British wives in the cantonment thought it beneath their dignity to gossip with servants, Mariam Labadoor, who made few social calls, enjoyed these conversations of hers. Often they enlivened her day by reporting the juiciest scandals, on which they were always well-informed. But from what Mariam had heard recently, she was convinced that it was only a matter of hours before rioting broke out in the city.[24]

It is this quality of hers that she is able to adjust in the house of Javed Khan and receive love of his aunt Kothiwali. She gives her introduction:

> The girl is Khurshid, my only daughter. My name is Mariam, and my family is well-known in Rampur, where my father was a minister of the Nawab.[25]

Javed's wife asks her which Rampur she is speaking about. Mariam's reply that she belongs to *Rohelon-ka-Rampur* impresses her and Kothiwali and they both begin to feel sympathy for her. Javed, too, is impressed and declares that he will marry Khurshid.

Her tactfulness saves Ruth on many occasions. The first occasion is when Javed proposes to marry Ruth, she first takes the plea that she is a Christian. But Javed says that a Pathan can marry a woman from any race or creed as his father and uncle did. Now she is silent. But soon she recovers her presence of mind and says:

> I trust you will not expect an immediate answer to your request. I have just lost my husband, and there is no one to guide or advise me. Let us speak again on this subject at some other time.[26]

These words of hers satisfies Javed and he says that he is not in a hurry and she can take a week for consultation and decision. Thus, she evades the problem. The second-time proposal is also delayed. Javed inquires of her:

> Mariam, you promised to speak to me again on a certain subject which you know is close to my heart. Now that you have time to think it over, perhaps you can give me a definite answer.[27]

But she feigns ignorance and wants to know the subject. Now Javed replies in very straightforward words that his proposal is to marry her daughter. Her reply is that she cannot think of her daughter's marriage in the present situation which is quite perilous. Sarfaraj came the other day to kill them. At this Javed says that there is no question of fear so long they are in his house. No person can enter his house and do any kind of mischief so long he is alive. Then Mariam takes the other plea that she must consult her relatives. Javed answers that they may have been killed.

The next pretext is that they should wait for the outcome of the war. Suppose the English Government is restored to power, what will they do then? His life will be worth little, and it may be that her daughter will be a widow at the age of thirteen. Therefore, she pleads, he should wait for a few months. But Javed refutes her arguments. He says that she is on the side of the English government and this is why she is speaking like that. She must know that only a few thousand white men are left and they can be wiped out in a short time. Secondly, if he wanted he could marry by force and she would be a dumb spectator.

These words of his terrify Mariam and she appeals to his good sense.

> Did I say you did not have that power? asked Mother. If you take her by force, we have no power to resist. But it would be unmanly of you to compel a fatherless child to gratify your desires. What merit would there be in that? Whereas, if you were to wait until the British are driven from Delhi, my argument would no longer carry any weight. And by that time, my daughter would be more of an age for marriage.[28]

He soon pacifies. Similarly, when Sarfaraz quarrels with Javed on their stay in the latter's house and both become so heated that they almost come to blows, Mariam comes straight between them and addresses Sarfaraz boldly:

> As to cutting off our heads...you have the power. Khan Saheb, and we cannot resist. If it should be Allah's will that we die by your hand, let it be so. There is but one favour, however, that I would ask of you, and that is that you kill every one of us, without exception. I shall not allow you to kill one or two only.[29]

Sarfaraz Khan is touched, both by her courage, and because she spoke in the name of Allah. He is calm now. He praises her faith and spirit:

> Great is your faith, and great your spirit.... Well, I wash my hands off this business. To have been sent on a fool's

errand, and to be put off by the calm persuasiveness of a woman!

It is her boldness, forbearance and persuasiveness that save her family's life, especially Ruth's and sustain them during the most troubled period in their life.

The world of the novel is essentially the world of women. In Labadoor's family, the principal figures are women: Mrs. Mariam Labadoor, Granny, Ruth, Anet, her mother, Pillo and Lado and Champa. The only male figure is Pillo who does not appear before us. When the Labadoor's family takes shelter in Ramjimal's house, all the people save Ramjimal are women. We hear their talk. Even when they go to Javed Khan's house, they meet women and women only. The only male figures are Javed Khan and occasionally Sarfaraz Khan. The women talk about things of their interest. Although they are well aware of the revolt, they are primarily concerned with their household duties, talking about other women and telling and listening to ghost stories.

It is really surprising that Ruskin Bond, a bachelor, has so much knowledge of the women world. Besides, his knowledge of Muslim culture is wonderful. He has used a number of Urdu words in the novel and described the customs of the Muslim community in detail. The speeches of Javed Khan and Kothiwali indicate Ruskin Bond's knowledge of Muslim beliefs and customs. Javed goes to hunt on Thursday. He injures a white pigeon. He falls ill on that day. He consults Abdul Rauf. Rauf says that pigeons are people who come out of their graves on Thursdays for a little fresh air. Javed believes him. After being shut in a room, he recovers. Then he says that the swelling on his face has been made by the slap given by the person in the grave.

The title *A Flight of Pigeons* is appropriate. Abdul Rauf Khan goes to pay respect to Mian Saheb, an old fakir and requests him to pray for the victory of their army. But Mian Saheb is wearing a mourning dress.

Abdul Rauf Khan reports. The fakir addresses him:

> "See, here they come!" he cried, pointing to north where a flock of white pigeons could be seen hovering over the city. They come flying like white pigeons which, when disturbed, fly away, and circle, and come down to rest again. White pigeons from the hills![30]

Here the pigeons are Ruth, Mariam, Granny, Anet, her mother, Pillo and his mother who are disturbed by the riots following the declaration of 1857 war and who fly like pigeons in a group but at last return their home, once the tumult subsides. They are common people, not people in power, and hence Indians like Javed Khan and Sarfaraz Khan.

The central figure is the tender girl Ruth of thirteen years. When birds or animals fly, the youngest are the objects of our sympathy. Ruth, being the youngest, wins our sympathy. She sees her father attacked and badly injured. She is Javed Khan's target. By European standard, no one can imagine a girl of thirteen to be married. Besides, the girl's consent is of the greatest importance. She resents, weeps and grieves over her helplessness. When we watch on Discovery Channel, the youngest deer pursued by a tiger or cheeta, as it cannot run fast, we are greatly moved. We watch with apprehension the run of Ruth's life and only when the war is over we heave a sigh of relief. The weakest and most delicate pigeon reaches home to our delight.

NOTES

1. *Ruskin Bond: Collected Fiction*, 898.
2. *Ibid.*, 825.
3. *Ibid.*, 828.
4. *Ibid.*, 831.
5. *Ibid.*, 834.
6. *Ibid.*
7. *Ibid.*, 840-41.
8. *Ibid.*, 842.
9. *Ibid.*, 878.
10. *Ibid.*, 835-36.
11. *Ibid.*, 836.
12. *Ibid.*, 837.
13. *Ibid.*, 846-47.

14. *Ibid.*, 851.
15. *Ibid.*, 849.
16. *Ibid.*
17. *Idem.*, 849.
18. *Ibid.*, 851.
19. *Ibid.*, 860.
20. *Ibid.*, 896.
21. *Idem.*, 896.
22. *Ibid.*, 832.
23. *Ibid.*, 846.
24. *Ibid.*, 827.
25. *Ibid.*, 848.
26. *Ibid.*, 851.
27. *Ibid.*, 859.
28. *Ibid.*, 861.
29. *Ibid.*, 859.
30. *Ibid.*, 871.

6

The Short Stories

This chapter is divided into two sections. In the first section are the stories written for children and the second, the stories for adolescents. This does not mean that the stories written for children cannot be read by adolescents or adults. *The Arabian Nights* are read by all and so are the first two journeys of Gulliver in simplified form. In fact there is no child who has not read *Gulliver in Liliput* and *The Adventures of Sindabad,* though *Gulliver's Travels* and *Alif Laila* (*The Arabian Nights*) are written for adults. However, Ruskin has written a large number of stories specially for children. The most significant shall be analysed one by one.

The Woman on Platform No. 8 is the first story in the *Collected Fiction.* Here the contrasting attitudes of two elderly women is presented through the narration of a boy of twelve, named Arun. At the age of twelve or nearly so Arun was going to his boarding school. He was to change his train at Ambala. Getting down at Ambala, he waited for the north bound train. His parents considered him old enough to travel alone. He had arrived by bus at the station and was waiting for the train that was to come at midnight. He saw the people boarding and getting down the trains, the helplessness of the ticket collector and the arrival and departure of trains. He paced up and down, fed dogs broken biscuits and looked here and there. At last, he got tired of everything and, so, sat down on his suitcase and gazed dismally across the railway gates.

Suddenly a sweet voice of an elderly woman broke his silence. He looked up and saw the woman with a pale face and dark kind eyes. She wore no jewels, and was dressed very simply in a white sari. He stood up respectfully and replied that he was going to school. She said that she had been watching him for sometime and wondering why he was alone. Then she asked if his parents had not come to the station to see him off. Arun answered that he had to change the train at Ambala and that he would come at midnight. The woman felt sympathy for him and took him to the other side of the platform and fed him with *samosa*, *jalebi* and tea. Her hospitality was hypnotising. He could not resist her offer. They talked for a long time. She spoke less and the boy more. Later on, his friend Satish came to the platform. He was with his mother. She thought that the woman with Arun was his mother. They talked and every time the mother of Satish warned them of the strangers. After sometime the train came and they bade goodbye.

The difference between a novel and short-story is that the former is about the whole life, or at least a large part of the life of the protagonist and other characters but the latter is concerned with a slice of the protagonist's life. This slice is a momentous event that changes the course or thought-process of her/his life. Here we find that a strange woman helps Arun, a young boy of about twelve. She is a compassionate woman. She is full of pity when she sees the boy all alone on the platform late at night. Her compassionate nature is further illustrated. An engine is shuttling. In the meantime a young boy tries to cross the track. This scene terrifies her. She is so immensely perturbed that she clutches Arun with all her force and her nails pierce his flesh. Satish's mother, on the other hand is a matter-of-fact woman. She advises him:

> Be very careful when your mother is not with you. And never talk to strangers.

She does not know that the woman beside Arun is a different woman. Arun reacts in a different way unwittingly and moves closer to the woman. He now understands that love and compassion are much above reason and mistrust.

"'Good-bye", I said to the woman, "good-bye Mother..."

I didn't wave or shout, but sat still in front of the window, gazing at the woman on the platform.[1]

The Coral Tree. If "The Woman on Platform No. 8" is the perception of a ten year old boy of the adult world, "The Coral Tree" is the perception of an adult of a small child. It is the general tendency of young children to travel wide and emulate elder people. In this story the narrator, an adult in twenties, meets a small girl standing in the veranda porch. She looks at him seriously. She is a small, dark girl, her eyes big and black and her pigtails are tied up in a bright red ribbon. He finds her fresh like the recent rain and the wet red earth. He greets her and she responds by nodding her head only as she is serious. A dialogue takes place between them. The dialogue reveals the fact that a small child wants to grow big and independent and act like an adult.

With great assurance she said, "yes. But I can stay on my own."

"You're like me," I said, and for a while I forgot about being an old man of twenty. "I like to do things on my own. I'm going away today."

"Oh, she said, a little breathlessly."

"Would you care to go to England?"

"I want to go everywhere she said, to America and Africa and Japan and Honolulu."

Soon the talk drops from the high pedestal to the base. The girl wants a bunch of flowers from the coral tree nearby. The narrator fulfils her demand. Now covered with coral flowers and glowing with the happiness of getting them the little child looks really fresh like the earth recently bathed in rain.

The Photograph is the third story in the collection narrated by a young boy of ten years. Told in a very simple way it hints at the fact that all children are naughty in the beginning of life and they become serious only at a late stage.

The narrator remembers an incident when he was ten years old. His grandmother sat on a cot under the mango before the house. It was late summer and the atmosphere was warm. She was very old. All her hair was white. The narrator, after returning from the cricket field took his meal and opened the box which his mother just brought from the attic. Nothing interested him among the contents of the box except a book with coloured pictures of flowers and butterflies. While he was going through the pages he saw an old pale photograph. It was the photograph of a girl standing against a wall and behind the wall there was nothing but the sky. But from the other side a pair of hands reached up, as though someone was going to climb the wall. Seeing the picture the narrator got inquisitive and wanted to know the person whose photograph it was.

He went straight to his grandmother to know something about the photograph. His grandmother, at first, pretended not to know the girl but later on said:

> Yes, I knew her...but she was a very wicked girl and I shouldn't tell you about her. But I'll tell you about the photograph. It was taken in your grandfather's house about sixty years ago. And that's the garden wall and over the wall there was a road going to town.

Then the boy asked about the hands clutching the wall. She replied that she had no idea about it. She then guessed that they might have been of the sweeper boy or the grandfather. The boy doubted that they were his grandfather's as his fingers were bony. But she did not remember whose hands they were. She went on giving the other details of the picture like the season, the air, the flowers and the surroundings. She remembered well that the girl in the picture had been quite naughty and adventurous.

> Most of the time, she hardly wore a thing. She used to go swimming in a muddy pool with a lot of ruffianly boys, and ride on the backs of buffaloes. No boy ever teased her, though, because she could kick and scratch and pull his hair off.[2]

The boy was not satisfied with her words. He wanted to know about the identity of the girl and of the hands. Soon he recognized that the girl in the picture was his grandmother because there was a similarity between the smiles of the two.

"I knew, because Grandmother still smiled in the same way, even though she didn't have as many teeth."

However, the mystery of the hands remained unsolved. In this short story, Ruskin has hinted at the truth that all children are alike. They are all naughty, playful and full of energy. It is only when they grow up that they begin to change. The grandmother was the same what the grandson is now.

Chachi's Funeral is a story about two children to be told to children. Adults may think it to be absurd but it is quite funny and entertaining for the young people of the age group 9 to 12 years.

There is a joint family consisting of a number of adults and children. Sunil is a small boy, bright, good-looking and ingenious. His parents go to office in the morning and he is left in the custody of his Chachi who has many children. Her children are not that lovely as Sunil is. Naturally she has grudge against him. He, too, is not happy with her and occasionally teases her indirectly. One day he goes to the kitchen in search of honey. The glass jar is at a height and the small boy hardly reaches it. He tries to push it with his fingers. Unfortunately, the honey jar tilts and falls down on the floor. It crashes with a sound. Chachi hears the sound and comes running to the kitchen. She comes so fast that Sunil has no time to escape. Now Chachi beats him three or four times with her slipper. Sunil hates her so much that he does not cry nor does he protest. He leaves the kitchen and goes to his secret place where he keeps his tools and playthings. He takes a knife and stabs it into the window frame which is made of wood.

While he is thinking of murdering his Chachi, his cousin Madhu, a girl of about twelve years, enters his secret place. She is Chachi's daughter. She asks him what he is doing. He tells her his anguish and the plan to stab Chachi in the middle of her heart. Then Madhu says that if he kills Chachi, the CID will come and arrest him. Sunil asks if he will be hanged for killing Chachi. Madhu replies that he will be sent to a boarding school. Now Sunil hates the boarding school. Then Madhu suggests a fool proof plan.

She makes a drawing of Chachi and asks Sunil to stab it. He does it three times. She says that Chachi is killed. Sunil is happy. The next step is to cremate her. They take a match box, light a stick and then burn the paper on which is drawn Chachi's figure. The final step is to float the ashes in the river. As there is no river nearby, Madhu suggests it to be thrown into the drain. Sunil does it gladly. Thus Chachi's funeral is complete.

But after this Sunil is unhappy. He feels sincerely that he should not have killed Chachi and burned her dead body. When he sees Chachi he goes to her and expresses his love for her. Chachi does not understand the reason for his strange behaviour but the love and sincerity in his eyes make her a different woman. She feels that he understands her and then she takes him to the kitchen.

The Tunnel is one of the most anthologised stories of Ruskin Bond. The great quality of the story is that it has a universal appeal. Written primarily for children, it makes a serious reading. There are altogether four characters: Ranji, Kishen Singh, the leopard and Ranji's father. The train and the tunnel are not characters but are as important as Edgan Heath in Hardy's *The Return of the Native.*

The boy Ranji has the great desire to see the spectacle of a train emerging from the tunnel which is at a short distance from his house. He takes a bicycle and goes to the tunnel in daytime. After sometime the train comes from the tunnel. The whole scene is spectacular and it makes a great impact on Ranji.

"A second or two later the steam-engine shot out of the tunnel, snorting and puffing like some green, black and gold dragon, some beautiful monster out of Ranji's dreams. Showering sparks right and left, it roared a challenge to the jungle.

Instinctively Ranji stepped back a few paces. Waves of hot steam struck him in the face. Even the trees seemed to flinch from the noise and heat."[3]

After watching the train pass Ranji enters the tunnel to see the other end. He moves slowly to the tunnel and enters it. He finds the tunnel getting darker and darker. Soon he finds that there is darkness all around him. He returns and comes to the mouth to examine if there is light on the other side. He sees a bright hole at the other end. Again he moves on the rails and reaches the other end. There is Kishen Singh, the watchman. His duty is to examine the tunnel before a train comes. There are two trains only. The day time train is a passenger and the night train is a mail train.

Kishen Singh inspects the rails and the tunnel twice everyday. If there is anything wrong, he puts a red flag on the track to warn the driver of the danger in the tunnel. When Ranji meets Kishen Singh, he is resting on his cot. Kishen Singh gives him a good idea of the tunnel and the forest. He tells about the leopard that roams in the forest. He boasts that the tunnel belongs to him and he has given it to the government on rent. Besides, the leopard is his own property. He has a dislike for the town as his pocket was picked there. For him the leopard is more benign than the wicked townspeople. Then he asks Ranji to stay with him so that he can see the mail train at night. Ranji replies that he will come next day after taking permission from his father.

Next day, he comes to Kishen Singh in the evening. Kishen Singh has been waiting for him. He makes tea and offers a cup to Ranji. Then they both go to the tunnel. The night mail train will pass through it in ten minutes. Suddenly, they hear a strange sound. Kishen Singh recognizes it. It is the sound of the leopard. He comes to realize the fact that the leopard is entering the tunnel. He fears the tragic end of the innocent animal. Now, there is only one way to save its life. He takes the lamp and enters the tunnel. Ranji follows him. They see the leopard sitting between the rails. Kishen shouts. His shout angers the animal. It stands and twitches its tail. Now both Kishen and Ranji shout together. Their voices echo and rumble in the tunnel. The leopard is scared and it goes away from the tunnel. Soon, the mail train comes with all its force but the leopard is at a safe distance. Ranji and Kishen Singh are happy that they have saved the life of an innocent animal.

This is a remarkable story. The sound of a steam-engine may be something normal for the people of plains as trains are innumerable but for the hill people it is an experience. For the young children, the first experience is enormous and exhilerating. It is also common among the village people to boast and brag before children. Kishen Singh too boasts of his power and wealth before Ranji.

Thirdly, and this is most important, it is the compassion of the hill people for the wild animals that wins our heart. The sophisticated rich people hunt the wild animals like deer, hog, leopard, tiger and lion. They are cruel to them. Besides, there are poachers who poison tigers and lions for money. In contrast, Kishen Singh saves the leopard's life.

Finally, Ruskin Bond's style is at its best in the story. The story begins with a rich description of the place.

"It was almost noon, and the jungle was very still, very silent. Heat waves shimmered along the railway embankment where it cut a path through the tall evergreen trees. The railway lines were two straight black serpents disappearing into the tunnel in the hillside."

The ending of the story is also superb.

"The train went into the tunnel and out again, it left the jungle behind and thundered across the endless plains. And Ranji stared out at the darkness, thinking of the lonely cutting in the forest, and the watchman with the lamp who would always remain a firefly for those travelling thousands, as he lit up the darkness for steam-engines and leopards."

It is really a glowing tribute to the insignificant watchman Kishen Singh, a petty worker with stupendous responsibility.

Apart from the stories analysed in short, other stories are of not great significance excepting the stories for the adolescent and about the adolescent discussed in this chapter. Many of the stories which are not discussed are a kind of reminiscence or the stories told near the fireplace in winter. Even the story "Masterji" seems rather "unreal". The time when Bond wrote short stories, teachers were seldom handcuffed, though it is true many refugees from West Punjab told the lie that their certificates were destroyed.

It is a credit to Bond that he has written short stories about Indian people in India. His perception of the northern hill people and love of the place places him above the Indian writers who write about India for the foreigners. The characters in Bond's short stories are simple people with low income. He sees their problems as if it is his. He seldom writes about the rich children.

His knowledge of child psychology is based upon observation and experience. The stories fulfil all the conditions of a short story, that is, they deal with only one important event, the characters are limited in number, the plot is knit neatly and the end leaves us with satisfaction. Every short story of his has a beginning, a middle and a satisfactory end. We shall see all these qualities better displayed in stories like "Time Stops at Shamli" and "Night Train at Deoli".

II

Bond's stories about the adolescent are partly based on his personal experiences or the experiences of the people whom he has known thoroughly. These stories are love stories and especially of unrequited love.

The main reason for writing stories of unrequited love is that he himself had frustrating experiences. He writes in the Epilogue of *Rain in the Mountains*:

> There were only two occasions in my life when I came really to getting married. Once in London, when I was twenty-one and infatuated with a very sweet and pretty Vietnamese girl, who promised me her hand until she met a rich American and found his signature more attractive than mine.[4]

But he writes about the same girl in a different way in *Scenes from a Writer's Life*.

> It was Thanh who introduced me to a Vietnamese girl called Vu-Phuong, and I promptly fell in love with her.

> At that age (of twenty) it did not take long for me to fall in love with anyone, and Vu was the sort of girl—pretty, soft-spoken, demure—who could enslave me without any apparent effort.[5]

The pages 152-53 of *Scenes from a Writer's Life* are devoted to his days with Vu and her picture is printed with other pictures between pages 80 and 81. The way their relation ended is quite differently narrated from what is said in *Rain in the Mountains*. The paragraph runs as follows:

> Two or three weeks later I asked Vu if she'd marry me. She didn't say yes and she didn't say no. Nor did she ask me if I had any prospects, because it was obvious I had none. But she did say she would have to talk to her parents about it and they were in Haiphong, in North Vietnam, and she hadn't heard from them for several months. The war in Vietnam had just started and it was to last a long time.
>
> I had to be patient, it seemed, very patient.
>
> Because the next I heard from Vu was through a postcard from Paris saying she was staying with her sister for a time and they would be returning to Vietnam together to see their parents.[6]

Bond's narrations of his broken love are contradictory. The long Vietnamese war made every Vietnamese a great hater of America. In that case it was impossible for Vu to marry an American and go to America. She could be suspected as a spy. Therefore, we can accept Bond's narration in *Scenes from a Writer's Life* as true and in *Rain in the Mountains* a kind of white lie.

His second love was Miss Bun about whom he writes:

> And the second time, when I met a nurse from Ferozepur, who made it her business to take charge of me for several months. She was a fine strapping girl, but I think I would have felt *sat upon* (literally too) if I had been yoked to her for life.[7]

The memoir entitled "Miss Bun and Others" printed in *Rain in Mountains* sketches Miss Bun as a baker's young daughter with whom the author makes love. By the language of the memoir we cannot say that he is in love with her. The age difference is vast:

> If you were ten years older, and I was ten years younger, we'd make a good pair.[8]

Later on, he concludes:

> These journal entries date back some twenty years. What happened to Miss Bun? Well, she finally opened a beauty parlour in New Delhi, but still I can't tell you where it is, or give you her name.[9]

We find that the author again has mixed two persons and given one name Miss Bun. The nurse is Miss Bun and here the baker's daughter is Miss Bun. They merge at the end in the beauty parlour. It is said that authors are seldom true in telling about their life and evaluating their contemporaries.

However, the female characters in Bond's love stories have their origin in Mrs. Lal, Vu and the Ferozepur nurse and may be some other young girl whose name he has never disclosed. His focus is always on a girl of thirteen.*

The first story "The Night Train at Deoli" is about the one-sided Platonic love of an adolescent for a basket-seller at Deoli station.

Deoli is a small station thirty miles away from Dehradun and the night train arrives at its platform early in the morning at five o'clock. Although the writer describes the station and its surroundings in detail, the Northern Railway time table does not mention it. By the distance, as the author gives us, the station should be between Dehradun and Haridwar but, in fact, there is no station named Deoli before or after Haridwar.

We can assume that it is a fictitious station or it may have existed when Ruskin Bond was young. However, we are not concerned with the existence of Deoli in our real world; it is a place enveloped by romance and mystery. The story begins with a description of the station:

---

* The basket selling girl in "The Night Train at Deoli", Madhu in "The Story of Madhu", Sushila when she reaches thirteen and Ruth in *A Flight of Pigeons*.

> The train would reach Deoli at about five in the morning when the station would be dimly lit with electric bulbs and oil lamps and the jungle across the railway tracks would just be visible in the faint light of dawn. Deoli had only one platform, an office for the station master and a waiting room. The platform boasted a tea stall, a fruit vendor, and a few stray dogs; not much else because the train stopped there for only ten minutes before rushing on into the forest.[10]

For the protagonist, who goes to Dehradun often to his old grandmother, the whole place is shrouded in mystery. First, he does not understand the reason why the train stops at the station at all. He never sees a passenger boarding the train nor any getting down from it. He wonders why the train stops for full ten minutes and what happens behind the station walls. He sometimes has the feeling to get down at Deoli, go beyond the station walls and stay in the town for a day.

But something happens one day. He goes to his grandmother's house and the train stops at Deoli as usual. This morning he sees a girl on the platform. She is selling baskets. She has a shawl thrown across her shoulder. She is without shoes or slippers and her clothes are old. In spite of her poverty, she is walking gracefully and with dignity. When she comes to his window, she stops. She does so because the protagonist has been watching her intently. Her pale skin, shiny black hair and dark troubled eyes fascinate him. She stands by his window for sometime. No one speaks. But as she starts moving away, he cannot resist himself and leaves his seat. He goes to the tea stall and waits there for sometime. In the meantime, the girl comes to him and asks him if he would like to buy a basket. His answer is in the negative but when the girl repeats, he says that he will buy one. He gives her a rupee. As she is about to speak, the guard blows the whistle. She says something but it is lost in the changing of the bell and the hissing of the engine. He runs back to his compartment. But the girl's face haunts his memory during the journey.

He forgets her during his two month's sojourn in his grandmother's house. But when he returns, he remembers the girl as the train reaches Deoli. He sees her walking up the platform. He is thrilled. She, too, smiles when she sees him.

> She was pleased that I remembered her. I was pleased that she remembered me. We were both pleased and it was almost meeting of old friends.
>
> She did not go down the length of the train selling baskets but came straight to the tea stall. Her dark eyes were suddenly filled with light. We said nothing for sometime but we couldn't have been more eloquent.[11]

He invites, in his adolescent and romantic way, to go with him to Delhi but the girl, like most of the girls of her age, replies that she cannot leave her place. The train whistles. He, this time, does not forget her and cherishes her in his memory. After reaching Delhi, he is busy in his studies and, after the examinations, goes to his grandmother's house at Dehradun. After reaching Deoli, he looks for the girl with searching eyes but she is not there. He inquires of the tea vendor and the stationmaster but their replies are meaningless for him. He becomes apprehensive about her. The train starts and he runs to his compartment.

> As Deoli platform recedes, he decides that one day he would break journey there, spend a day in the town, make inquiries, and find the girl who had stolen my heart with nothing but a look from her dark, impatient eyes.[12]

But an adolescent that he is, he does not drop down there to make a search for the girl whom he loves. He fears something worse—prolonged illness, marriage or permanent departure. He makes this comment perhaps with a wry smile:

> Somehow, I couldn't bring myself to break journey at Deoli and spend a day there. (If it was all fiction or film, I reflected I would have got down and cleaned up the mystery and reached a suitable ending for the whole thing.) I think I was afraid to do this. I was afraid of discovering what really happened to the girl. Perhaps, she was no longer in Deoli, perhaps she was married, perhaps she had fallen ill....[13]

The story ends with the protagonist's hope to see the girl. But this hope is feeble and is mixed with fear. He does not have the courage to face the unpleasant, if it is there. He passes through Deoli often and whenever, the platform comes near, he hopefully looks through the window to see the smiling face. He does not have the courage to cross over the boundary wall of the station and go to the town to find her out or at least know her whereabouts. All that he does is to look through the window if he will see her smiling face some day. He wants to keep his dream alive; the memory of the two mornings must remain fresh in his mind.

This story as we see it is about an adolescent of eighteen years studying in a college. An adolescent falls in love very easily. In fact, every adolescent is dreamy and dreams of beautiful and noble things. Besides, he or she, on the verge of entrance to the adult world, wants to love someone and be loved by someone. Beauty and youth play a great role here. This is what happens to the protagonist. We may call it "love at first sight", but it is true. Bond has put his own perception of life in this passage which contains his poem "Passing By".

As a youth, loneliness always went hand in hand with a powerful pull or attraction towards another person, be it a boy or girl—and very often without that individual being aware of it. I think I expressed this feeling in a short poem "Passing By", which I wrote many years ago:

Enough for me that you are beautiful:
Beauty possessed diminishes,
Better a dream of love
Than love's dream broken;
Better a look exchanged
Than love's word spoken
Enough for me that you walk past,
A firefly flashing in the dark.[14]

This story "Night Train at Deoli" is a dream of love. The adolescent does not want his dream to be broken and so, he never dares to drop at the station and go to the town to inquire into the whereabouts of the girl.

Love is a Sad Song is a long short story. Apparently, this story is on the pattern of Vladimir Nabokov's infamous novel *Lolita* where the protagonist, an aged man, marries the minor girl's mother in order to have Lolita when she grows to maturity. The age difference is there and will remain so even if Lolita reaches the age of eighteen but uneven marriages are permitted in the amoral American society.

In this story, too, there is the age difference; the protagonist is thirty and the girl with whom he establishes sex relationship is sixteen and like the protagonist of *Lolita* has to wait for two years when the girl, Sushila, will be eighteen. The story according to Dr. Naikar,

> ...is a lyrical novella or long short story depicting the ups and downs of uneven love between the protagonist and a young girl called Sushila.... Viewed against the Indian context, the protagonist is too old to be a lover and Sushila, too young to be a beloved. But yet [sic] the contingencies [sic] of their life awaken in them an emotional attraction for each other.[15]

It is difficult to agree with Dr. Naikar when he calls this story a "lyrical novella". It is a short story, a bit long, but not a novella. The language is poetic but this does not mean that it is a "lyrical novella" as we speak of an opera or lyrical drama. Besides, he is off the point when he says, "Viewed against the Indian context, the protagonist is too old to be a lover and Sushila, too young to be a beloved." In fact, he has mixed the words husband and lover confusedly and in the same manner the words wife and beloved. The protagonist and Sushila are already in love and have sexual union; age is the bar between their nuptial union. Besides, he should have used the word "exigency" not "contingency" and "but" and "yet" do not come together.

The story, as said earlier, is a love story which does not end in the happy marriage between the protagonist and Sushila, the latter being a girl of sixteen years only; the protagonist has to wait two years more with a trembling heart and the fear that she may change her mind for a rich husband. Her fickleness has already been known to him by her previous boy-friend's letter and the arrival of Pramod, her another lover; she changes her friends often and may desert him for a lover who owns a car.*

Troubled by these problems, the narrator or protagonist addresses Sushila expressing his emotions and remembering the happy days he has spent with her. The first three pages are charged with emotion. The opening paragraphs are highly poetic and remind us of Goethe's *Meister Wilhelm* and *Lott in Mar*. I quote the first two paragraphs:

> I sit against this grey rock, beneath a sky of pristine blueness and think of you Sushila. It is November and the grass is turning brown and yellow. Crushed, it still smells sweet. The afternoon sun shimmers on the oak leaves and turns them a glittering silver. A cricket sizzles its way through the long grass. The stream murmurs at the bottom of the hill—that stream where you and I lingered on a golden afternoon in May.
>
> I sit here and think of you and try to see your slim brown hand resting against this rock, feeling its warmth. I am aware again of the texture of your skin, the coolness of your feet, the sharp tingle of your fingertips. And in the pastures of my mind I run my hand over your quivering mouth and crush your tender breasts. Remembered passion grows sweeter with the passing of time.[16]

The paragraphs describe the autumnal beauty in the mountains of North India. The whole scene is picturesque: the grey rock, the clear blue sky, the brown and yellow grass, the glittering oak leaves in the afternoon sun of November, the sizzling cricket and the murmuring stream in the golden afternoon hypnotize the reader. Against this backdrop the narrator sits and thinks of his beloved Sushila and imagines her sitting by the grey rock like the Lady of the Rock. He remembers her beauty and the way his passion is quenched by

---

* Sushila marries Dayal, a hotel owner (Vide "Time Stops in Shamli"). Bond's comments on Vu (already quoted) are relevant here.

her. The lines move rhythmically and they can be easily broken into lines of poetry. For example, the first three sentences:

I sit against this grey rock,
Beneath a sky of pristine beauty,
And think of you, Sushila. It is
November and the grass
Is turning brown and yellow.
Crushed, it still smells sweet.

Bond sustains this poetic rhythm for many pages and if dialogues are there, they appear to be dialogues between dancing partners in an opera.

It is through the narrator's recollection of the past that the story of his love is revealed to us. He imagines her to be away in her home in the city doing her household duties like cooking or sewing or, may be, studying for her examinations. She must be busy with the members of her family but, he hopes, she would be thinking of him in her private moments when she is all alone in her house.

We come to know that he was acquainted with Sushila when she was ten only. At that time she was a simple girl and he had fatherly affection for her. He had seen her naked playing in rain; he never thought of loving her. But once she reached sixteen, he found changes in her:

> A year ago my feelings about you were almost paternal! Or so I thought.... But you are no longer a child and I am a little older too. For when, the night after the picnic, you took my hand and held it against your warm soft cheek, it was the first time that a girl had responded to me so readily, so tenderly. Perhaps, it was just innocence but that one action of yours, that acceptance of me, immediately devastated my heart.[17]

His mention of the picnic reminds us of the picnic in *The Room on the Roof* and Rusty's kissing of Mrs. Meena Kapoor and her response. Here we find the same scene replicated in a slightly different way, the sixteen year girl almost passive.

> Gently, fervently, I kissed your eyes and forehead, your small round mouth, and the lobes of your ears, and your long smooth throat; and I whispered, "Sushila, I love you, I love you, I love you" in the same way that millions and millions of love-smitten young men have whispered since time immemorial.... I was a man and yet I was a boy again.[18]

The intensity of feeling is deep and we admire it. But what makes us suspect Bond's sincerity is the reversal of the scene in *The Room on the Roof*. In *The Room on the Roof* there is Kishen and his mother Meena Kapoor and Kishen partly knows the love relationship between his mother and Rusty but, surprisingly, he accepts it. For we Indians in the nineteen fifties it was blasphemous. Here, too, the role is changed. There was Meena Kapoor almost twice older than Rusty and here is the narrator twice older than Sushila. Sunil, like Kishen, is twelve years old. Love, we find, is purely physical: a man of thirty exploits a teenager, a crime even by western standards.

Now coming to the narration, we see that the author introduces the element of sadness. After the picnic they return home. When they go for a stroll after dinner on a dark road Sunil knowing their intimacy takes his hand and puts it in Sushila's hand. Sushila, then, asks him to tell a story. Sunil, too, demands the same thing. The narrator tells a sad story and calls it a story of the pure in heart.

> A shepherd boy found a snake in the forest and the snake told the boy that it was really a princess who had been bewitched and turned into a snake and that it could only recover its human form if someone who was truly pure in heart gave it three kisses on the mouth. The boy put his lips to the mouth of the snake and kissed it thrice. And the snake was transformed into a beautiful princess. But the boy lay cold and dead.[19]

Sunil does not like the story as it is sad. But it expresses indirectly the sadness of the narrator who fears the separation from Sushila.

In his random recollections, he recounts how he felt jealousy when she told him that a boy friend of hers shifted his love from a girl to her. Her words arouse jealousy in his heart and then he remembers the passionate moments he spent with her, the moments when they became one and Sushila demanded more and more love.

> We sat together at the foot of your bed. I kept my arm about you, while you rested your head against my chest. Your feet lay in repose upon mine. I kept kissing you. And when we lay down together, I loosened your blouse and kissed your small firm breasts, and put my lips to your nipples and felt them grow hard against my mouth.
>
> The shy responsiveness of your kisses soon turned to passion. You clung to me. We had forgotten time and place and circumstance. The light of your eyes had been drowned in that lost look of a woman who desires. For a space we both struggled against desire. Suddenly I had become afraid of myself—afraid for you. I tried to free myself from your clasping arms. But you cried in a low voice, "Love me! Love me! I want you to love me."[20]

This transformation to womanhood at the age of sixteen is rather Indian. The whole of Indian amorous and erotic literature is about the *Shodashi Naika** (sixteen-year-old heroine). Here also, the simple school girl becomes the object of love of a thirty-year-old man and acts as a full-fledged young woman of twenty-one or twenty-two. The contrast between the child and the adolescent is quite sharp and the change in the body and psyche is surprising. The protagonist recollects Sushila's early years.

> I tried to remember what you looked like as a child. Even then, I had always been aware of your presence. You must have been nine or ten when I first saw you—thin, dark, plain-faced, always wearing the faded green skirt that was your school uniform. You went about barefoot. Once, when the monsoon arrived, you ran out into the rain with the other children, naked, exulting in the swish of the cool rain. I remembered your beautiful straight legs and thighs, your swift smile, your dark eyes. You say you do not remember playing naked in the rain but that is because you did not see yourself.

* Also *Bala* meaning young woman. *Balika* means girl.

I did not notice you growing. Your face did not change very much. You must have been thirteen when you gave up skirts and started wearing the salwar-kameez. You had few clothes but the plainness of your dress only seemed to bring out your own radiance. And as you grew older, your eyes became more graceful. And then, when you came to me in the hills, I found that you had been transformed into a fairy princess of devastating charm.[21]

The physical changes that come to a child while crossing the threshold of adolescence are marked by adult people, though the child is not fully aware of them. It is the comment of the elderly people that awakes the child and makes her or him realize that he or she is a child no more. The protagonist notices the changes in Sushila of which she is hardly aware. She is also not fully aware of what she looks like at the age of sixteen but for the narrator she is a grown up woman.

However, the narrator's love is purely sexual. It centres round the body of Sushila. He does not bother about her other qualities. This makes the difference between the great German poet and novelist Goethe and Ruskin Bond. Bond does not reach even the height of Tennyson in *Maud*. Love is far above flesh or sex.

Once, when they are lying in bed in one another's arms, Dinesh, the twenty-three years old uncle of Sushila enters the room. He is surprised but does not say any harsh words. Realizing his guilt the narrator (and here we come to know that he is an Anglo-Indian and is unaware of the Indian tradition) goes to Dinesh and tells that he wants to marry her. Dinesh at first disbelieves him but later on relents and then speaks of the problems that are there as hurdles in the marriage. The great problem is the age difference between the narrator and Sushila and the greater is that Sushila is underage by two years, the minimum age of marriage of a girl being eighteen. Then there is his elder brother Ravi and above all the grandmother whose words will be final.

Before the matter is settled, Sushila's another lover, Pramod meets him. He is twenty-three and nearer to Sushila's age. At first, he is jealous of Pramod but later on, recognizing his simplicity and innocence, feels sympathy for him.

He receives the final words from Ravi that marriage is not possible as Sushila is underage. He addresses Sushila:

> Listen Sushila, the worst has happened. Ravi has written to say that a marriage will not be possible—not now, not next year; never. Of course, he makes a lot of excuses—that you must receive a complete college education ("higher studies"), that the difference in our age is too great, that you might change your mind after a year or two—but reading between the lines, I can guess that the real reason is your grandmother.[22]

The story practically ends here but the narrator makes a few digressions and Sushila's words that he should wait. The digressions are unnecessary. The sentence that closes the story should have come earlier:

> I may stop loving you, Sushila but I will never stop loving the days I loved you.[23]

The ending sentence just quoted is rather vague. What does the narrator mean by "I will never stop loving the days I loved you"? If he stops loving Sushila, the days he spent with her will not be loving. On the other hand, the girl would be a kind of whore who gave him some pleasure. The sentence contains wit but not meaning.

In fact, though it is titled *Love is a Sad Song,* it is not a love story or song in the true sense of the word. It is a story of a pervert man who exploited a teenager for his sexual satisfaction and this is why the ending sentence is vague and lacks the intensity of feeling and sincerity of emotion. The way it begins it does not progress and often there are lapses in prose and dialogues in conversational language. It is a potboiler written by a man for the adolescents of immature minds like most of the boy-and-girl Hindi films.

Time Stops at Shamli may be said to be a sequel of *Love is a Sad Song*. Here, the female protagonist is Sushila, married to a rich person in Shamli. Shamli, in reality, is a small town on Delhi-Saharanpur railway route. But the author places it near

Dehradun. In fact, Deoli in the story "The Night Train at Deoli" is Shamli in *Time Stops at Shamli*. Let us compare the descriptions of these two places.

1. The Night Train at Deoli—Deoli was a small station about thirty miles from Dehradun. It marked the beginning of the heavy jungles of the Indian Terai.

The train would reach Deoli at about five in the morning when the station would be dimly lit with electric bulbs and oil lamps and the jungle across the railway tracks would just be visible in the faint light of dawn. Deoli had only one platform, an office for the stationmaster and a waiting room. The platform boasted a tea stall, a fruit vendor, and a few stray dogs; not much else because the train stopped there for only ten minutes before rushing on into the forests.

Why it stopped at Deoli, I don't know. Nothing ever happened there. Nobody got off the train and nobody got in. There were never any coolies on the platform. But the train would halt there a full ten minutes and then a bell would sound, the guard would blow his whistle, and presently Deoli would be left behind and forgotten.

I used to wonder what happened in Deoli behind the station walls. I always felt sorry for that lonely little platform and for the place that nobody wanted to visit.

2. Time Stops at Shamli—The Dehradun Express usually drew into Shamli at about five o'clock in the morning at which time the station would be dimly lit and the jungle across the tracks would just be visible in the faint light of dawn. Shamli is a small station at the foot of the Siwalik hills and it lies at the foot of the Himalayas which in turn lie at the feet of God.

The station, I remember, had only one platform, an office for the stationmaster, and a waiting-room. The platform boasted a tea stall, a fruit vendor, and a few stray dogs. Not much else was required because the train stopped at Shamli for only five minutes before rushing on into the forests.

Why it stopped at Shamli, I never could tell. Nobody got off the train and nobody got in. There were never coolies on the platform. But the train would stand there a full five minutes and the guard would blow his whistle and presently Shamli would be left behind and forgotten....[24]

The description of the two stations is identical. Not only this, even the words of the second paragraph in the two passages are not altered. Only the train stops for five minutes in Shamli but ten minutes at Deoli. Why has Bond repeated the same words in the opening paragraphs is a mystery? Is it the failure of imagination? Or is it that the place, may be Raiwala, is a part of his personal experience where he unconsciously returns?

It is also that both the stories are among his best. Perhaps, *Time Stops at Shamli* is his best short story; in fact, his longest. The protagonist does not get down at Deoli because he has a happy dream which he does not want to be broken by visiting the small town and trace out the basket-seller. Here, he, a mature man of thirty-five goes to Shamli and faces the reality of life and experiences it.

Dr. Murari Prasad quotes Bond's comments on *Time Stops at Shamli* in this connection:

> Small towns do not change in the way that cities change. It is still possible to find the old landmarks and sometimes the old people. There is a timelessness about small-town and cantonment India that I have tried to capture in a story like *Time Stops at Shamli.* It begins like "The Night Train at Deoli" in my earlier collection, but this time I step off the train, explore the place, discover a boarding house inhabited by a number of lonely individuals living in a time capsule like my own, meet an old love, and discover a few things about myself before continuing my journey.[25]

Bond is all right here. But what I feel is that some unbreakable bond is there with this place which brings him time and again to it. Let us take another passage; this time from *Delhi is Not Far*. Here is Kamla living in a village near Pipalnagar:

> I waited behind some trees on the outskirts of the village until I saw her playing with a little boy. Then I whistled and stepped out of the trees but when she saw me she

motioned me back and took the child into one of the small mud houses.

I waited amongst the sal trees until I heard footsteps a short distance away.

"Where are you?" I called but received no answer. I walked in the direction of the door steps and found a small path going through the trees. After a short distance the path turned to meet a stream and Kamla was waiting there.

"Why didn't you wait for me?" I asked.

"I wanted to see if you would follow me."

"Well I am good at it", I said, sitting down beside her on the banks of the stream.[26]

Kamla's behaviour is somewhat unusual and so are her words. Now let us read this passage from *Time Stops at Shamli*:

I walked back through the trees, but I couldn't find Sushila.

"Sushila where are you?" I called, but I might have been speaking to the trees, for I had no reply. There was a small path going through the orchard, and on the path I saw a rose petal. I walked a little further and saw another petal. They were from Sushila's red rose.... The path bent to meet a stream, there was a willow coming down to the water's edge, and Sushila was waiting there.

"Why didn't you wait?" I said.

"I wanted to see if you were as good at following me as you used to be."

"Well, I am", I said, sitting down beside her on the grassy bank of the stream.[27]

This is almost a replication of the scene of meeting with Kamla in *Delhi is Not Far*.

By quoting these passages and linking the female figures—the basket-selling girl at Deoli, Kamla, a prostitute and Sushila of *Love is a Sad Song* and of Shamli—my purpose is to bring out the deep-rooted feeling of loneliness in Ruskin Bond. In actual life as we discussed in the beginning of this chapter his frustration in love with Miss Bun (maybe the fictitious name of the nurse in Ferozepur) the Vietnamese girl Vu and the elderly lady Mrs. Lal.

As said earlier, this short story is a sequel of *Love is a Sad Song* but it is far superior to its predecessor in technique and treatment of the theme. The beginning of the story is full of mystery and it appetizes our curiosity. Once the narrator hires a tonga and is told there is a sugar factory and a less frequented hotel owned by Mr. Dayal we begin to feel that we are being led to an unknown place, the mystery of which may surprise us.

The tonga is the only tonga that carries people from the town to the station and from the station to the town. He gets into the tonga. The boy takes him to Shamli town. After crossing a forest they reach a bungalow which the tongawalah calls a hotel. There are a few houses nearby and a sugar factory which is the cause of Shamli's existence. It is six o'clock in the morning and all the inmates are asleep. The narrator pays one rupee to the tongawalah and waits patiently on the verandah. He sees a young man taking bath, after waiting for sometime. He is the caretaker, bearer and cook all together. The narrator addresses him to draw his attention. The young man whose name is Dayaram smiles slowly but sincerely and then asks if he has come to stay. The narrator answers that he has come to stay for a day. Dayaram shows him the room where he can stay and then asks if he wanted something to eat immediately; the usual time of breakfast is eight o'clock, he says. The narrator wants to have bath and change his clothes; so, he replies that he will have his breakfast with other people.

During his talk with Dayaram he learns that Mr. Dayal is the manager of the hotel. He is not highly educated and is a kind of unsuccessful man. So his father, the owner of the hotel, made him the manager. Then the narrator goes to his room which is spacious and comfortable and its window opens at the large field and garden outside. When he opens the window, he sees a young girl of ten playing on the swing. He goes to her, asks her name and pushes the swing for her. The girl, whose name is Kiran, is open and talkative like the girls of her age.

She expresses her opinion frankly about the place and the people when asked. Heera is a gardener, very old nearly hundred, Dayaram is her bodyguard, her father is the manager of the factory, Mr. Dayal is mean, Mrs. Dayal is generous and the guests in the hotel are Mr. Lin and Miss Deeds. Her frankness surprises the narrator. He comments:

> I was fascinated by Kiran's *ruthless summing up* of the guests.[28] (Italics mine)

He returns to the hotel. He hears sweet music played on piano. Entering the room he finds Mr. Lin, with his typical Mongolian features, playing the musical instrument. His entrance into the room does not surprise Mr. Lin. After the preliminary introduction both tell lies. The narrator asks about the music Lin is playing. Lin answers that it is Chopin. Lin has come to Shamli on a business purpose. He has to make a deal with the sugar factory. While they are talking the bell rings for breakfast. They go there. There is Mr. Satish Dayal, the manager, already seated. The narrator says that he is an author. The whole atmosphere is of a house, not of a hotel. In the meantime Miss Deeds enters, a woman of thirty-five.

> She had on [sic] a skirt and blouse which accentuated a firm well-rounded figure, and she walked on high heels, with a rhythmical swaying of the hips. She had an uninteresting face, camouflaged with lipstick, rouge and powder—the powder so thick that it had become embedded in the natural lines of her face—but her figure compelled admiration.[29]

The talk is begun by Miss Deeds. She asks the narrator what he does and he replies that he is an author. She further asks if he is married. He answers that he is not and then puts the same question to her. She is not offended and then remarks that it seems everybody is unmarried in the hotel. Satish Dayal contradicts her by saying that he is married. After this the narrator is asked about his purpose of visiting Shamli. He, as he has already thought, replies that he has come to see Major Roberts who was at Shamli about three years ago. Lin sees through his deception and says that he knows Major Roberts. In the talk that follows both try to outwit the other to our great amusement. We can say that it is a kind of small talk. The atmosphere is sunny.

They hear the news that Heera's dog has been taken away by a leopard. This news makes them alert. The narrator and Satish Dayal come to the garden, observe the pug marks of the beast and decide to hunt it in the forest. The expedition is more a fun than a hunt. The gun that Satish carries is very old and, so, the narrator advises him to carry a lathi instead of the rusted gun. Being a simpleton, he takes a lathi and instructs others to carry more lathis. Lin refuses to go to the forest and Miss Deeds is not asked to accompany them as it would be a useless attempt to persuade her to come along with them. They go on watching the pug marks. After ten minutes they reach the riverbed. Then they enter the jungle; Satish Dayal, out of fear, is the last in the line. The atmosphere is heavy and humid and there is complete silence. A parrot screams suddenly. Satish Dayal is really terrified and asks Dayaram and the narrator to go back home immediately. He returns with Dayaram to the hotel. But the narrator stays and goes on. At last he reaches a stream. He enters into it and bathes. Coming out of the stream, he dries himself and sleeps. By the time he wakes, Dayaram comes back. They return with some delay. Dayaram speaks about the mystery of Miss Deeds recounting her past history. For the narrator Shamli is a place of mystery. He thinks:

> In a few hours…the tonga will come for me and I will be back at the station. The mysterious charm of Shamli will be no more, but whenever I pass this way I will wonder about these people, about Miss Deeds and Lin and Mrs. Dayal.
>
> Mrs. Dayal…. She was the one person I had yet to meet. It was with some excitement and curiosity that I looked forward to meeting her; she was about the only mystery left in Shamli, now, and perhaps she would be no mystery when I met her. And yet...I felt that perhaps she would justify the impulse that made me get down from the train.[30]

The curtain of Mrs. Dayal's mystery rises next day. He sleeps in the garden and when he wakes in the morning, he sees the swing moving slowly. He expects the person sitting on the swing to be Kiran but, to his surprise, she is a young woman; she is his beloved Sushila smiling at him. At first he thinks that he is dreaming but soon realizes that Sushila in reality is before him. Coming back to his own self he asks about her marriage and present life and if she is happy at Shamli. Sushila replies:

> I have been here two years, and I am already feeling old. I keep remembering our home—how young I was, how happy—and I am all alone with memories. But now you are here! It was a bit of magic.[31]

They talk and, later on, go to the stream and kiss each other. They lie silently on the green grass. As already the quoted passage shows, the old scene with Kamla is repeated here. They rise when the rain comes. The narrator asks Sushila to go with him but her reply is just like Kamla's: she is married and must be with her husband, though she may not love him and may remain unhappy all through her life.

> I am not happy and I do not love him, but neither am I so unhappy that I should hate him. Sometimes, for our own sake, we have to think of the happiness of others. What happiness would we have living in hiding from everyone we once knew and cared for. Don't be a fool. I am always here and you can come to see me, and nobody will be made unhappy by it. But take me away and we will only have regrets.[32]

Next day he goes to the station. He waits for Sushila but she does not come. These are his final thoughts:

> Somehow, I was not disappointed. I had never really expected her to come. Unattainable, Sushila would always be more bewitching and beautiful than if she were mine.
>
> Shamli would always be there. And I could always come back, looking for Major Roberts.[33]

Time Stops at Shamli is superb in technique, treatment of theme and use of language. The author slowly and gradually builds the atmosphere before the meeting between the narrator and Sushila takes place. We are hardly aware of the kind of place Shamli is. Deoli and Shamli are the same place. The narrator in the first story fears that the basket-selling girl might be married or dead but here he gets down at the station and proceeds to the town impulsively.

It is a small town sandwiched between two forests. The hotel is a very old bungalow, constructed in the Victorian era, and hence slightly mysterious in appearance. The dwellers are equally quaint in their behaviour. Lin is a man from Singapore, now living in Calcutta. Miss Deeds is an old maid, frustrated in love and suffering from loneliness. We are introduced to them slowly and thus the author builds the atmosphere gradually. Sushila is deliberately kept apart for a long time. Here he adopts the technique of Shakespeare. Shakespeare does not bring the tragic hero on the stage in the opening scene.

Sushila's arrival surprises us all and slowly we realize that she is the Sushila of *Love is a Sad Song;* references to Sunil, Delhi and Pramod confirm our anticipation. The end is superb. Sushila does not come to the station to go with him and the only solace for him is that he can come to Shamli whenever he wishes and though Sushila cannot be his wife, she will continue to love him.

It may be asked why Kiran, the ten-year-old girl, is included in the plot of *Time Stops at Shamli.* The answer is that she is Sushila when the latter was ten years old. The narrator goes to the swing to see Kiran and finds that there is Sushila at the place of the small girl. In other words, Kiran is now transformed in the adolescent Sushila, adolescent because she is only eighteen now.

"The Story of Madhu" is a tragic story. It can be compared to Rabindranath Tagore's "Home coming". In Tagore's short story the adolescent finds it impossible to adjust himself in the artificial environment of Calcutta and longs for going home to his mother. When he is not allowed, he runs away, gets drenched in rain, suffers from pneumonia and dies leaving his mother, brother and maternal uncle sad. Here, too, Madhu is unable to bear the separation, suffers from an inexplicable disease and dies.

The narrator recalls the days when he was in his late twenties and living in a town near the Himalyan foothills. At that time his outlook of life was still quite romantic. He liked the solitude of the little town, which he did not find in the cities. He used to sit under an old mango tree, with a notebook or a sketch pad on his knees. One morning, he sees a small girl of about nine, wearing torn clothes but very active in play. Slowly, an acquaintance grows between him and the girl whose name is Madhu and this is because he loves children. Madhu lives with an old woman whom she calls grandmother. She, in fact, is an orphan whom the poor old woman adopted as her grand-daughter. They live in penury. The narrator feels compassion and begins to help her in many ways. He wants her to stand on her own feet and, so, teaches her reading and writing and provides the reading and writing materials, and a teacher for her.

When she reaches the age of thirteen, she remains unaware of the physical changes in her but the narrator, being an adult, knows that some distance has to be maintained. He says:

> Three years glided imperceptibly, and at the age of thirteen Madhu was on the verge of blossoming into a woman. I began to feel a certain responsibility towards her.
>
> It was dangerous, I knew, to allow a child so pretty to live almost alone and unprotected, and to run unrestrained about the grounds. And in a censorious society she would be made to suffer if she spent too much time in my company.[34]

The decision to separate her from him and send her to a boarding school breaks Madhu's heart. Being an adolescent in the zero stage she does not understand why she is being sent away.

> But why... I can learn more from you, and from the teacher who comes. I am so happy here.[35]

His reply is:

> You will meet other girls and make many friends.... I will come to see you. And when you come home, we will be even happier. It is good that you should go.[36]

She falls seriously ill. The narrator visits her small hut. He finds that she has treasured all his gifts, even the ribbon he once playfully tied on her arms. He touches her hand. She recognizes the touch and smiles. The talk starts:

> "What will we do now?" she said, "When will you send me to school?"
>
> "Not for a long time. First you must get well and strong. That is all that matters."[37]

She does not hear his words. She knows that she is going to die. She asks:

> "Who will read to you under the tree?"... "Who will look after you?"[38]

The story ends with Madhu's life and ends the narrator's happiness:

> You will Madhu. You are grown up now. There will be no one else to look after me.
>
> The old woman was standing at my shoulder. A hundred years—and little Madhu was slipping away. The woman took Madhu's hand from mine, and laid it gently down. I sat by the cot a little longer, and then rose to go, all the loneliness in the world pressing upon my heart.[39]

This short story narrated by an adult about an adolescent is not only touching and technically perfect but also a true depiction of the adolescent heart and emotions. An adolescent is still unaware of the ways of the world. He or she is emotionally tied to his or her near and dear. Madhu is unable to resist the shock she suffers when she is told that she will go to a boarding school. The adult people must know the working of an adolescent's mind. The narrator realizes the truth after Madhu's saddening death.

The four stories analysed in this chapter are Bond's best about the adolescent. "The Night Train at Deoli" is about the hesitant adolescent girl and the hopeful adolescent lover. The second *Love is a Sad Song* is about the adolescent who is under the control of conventions. *Time Stops at Shamli,* decidedly a love story like its predecessor, depicts the conflict between tradition and love and "The Story of Madhu" indirectly touches the same theme of the conflict between convention and love and directly on the functioning of the adolescent mind and heart.

The Sensualist is a novella of forty-six pages with two major characters, the narrator and the recluse. The setting of the novel is in the foothills of the Himalayas, far away from the heat and dust of the plains. Since, Ruskin Bond is more familiar with the Garhwal and Kumaon area (now Uttarakhand), all his novels, excepting *A Flight of Pigeons,* have settings here. Most of the characters are either hill people or people who have settled permanently in Garhwal and Kumaon.

Ruskin Bond has chosen an isolated place in the Himalayas for a specific purpose in this novella. Most of the sages and hermits take shelter in the Himalayas to avoid the din and bustle of the town life and meditate without disturbance in the tranquillity of the caves in the mountains. The second character, the recluse, has abandoned the human society and taken shelter in a cave after his frustrating experience in life.

The novella begins with a quotation from the eighth century writer Damodar Gupta's *The Lessons of Love.*

> When you hold him in your two hands, you should first honour him duly and then devour him. You will find him with flesh upon his bones, but leave him as the remnants of a fish, which are spines and skin. But what am I saying? Even when there is no fish left, you shall by no means cast the bones aside till you have cracked them and sucked the marrow. He must be left incapable of work, unable even to stumble, with wandering glances, emptied, broken, finished....

The quotation gives the reader the hope that the story will build on this theme but, unfortunately, Bond gives a potboiler, a novella verging on pornography. The story begins with a promise but falls in the middle with a thud. The first two pages have a lively depiction of the hill area. The narrator is going to the village named Kapila which is nearby a river. He walks on foot and reaches the dry hills. The entire scene is described in simple but austere words.

> This range is bare and rocky, with steep hillsides suddenly rearing up in front of the tired, discouraged traveller. The grass is short and almost colourless. An eagle circles high overhead and the burning sun, striking through the rarefied

> atmosphere, is reflected from the granite rocks. Caves of banded light shimmer along the dusty mountain path. I walk alone and I am thirsty.[40]

The narrator looks behind at the valley he has left. The ascent is steep and the place is unfamiliar. It seems that people seldom come to this area. What is more disturbing is that it is three o'clock and the sun has started to go down. Evenings come early in September. Then he sees a small stream, goes there and washes his face. He sees that the path of the stream is man-made. Now he is sure that there must be some man near the top of the hill. He goes up and sees a cave and just at the mouth of the cave a black body. He cannot discern whether that object is an animal or a man. Later on, he finds that he is a man, lean and thin, wearing a loin-cloth. He is the recluse.

The recluse welcomes him. He says that he influenced the narrator's mind to lose the right path and come to him as he wanted some company. The narrator, earlier scared, is now confident and decides to spend the night in the cave of the recluse. Here, in the cave, the recluse tells the story of his sensual life.

His first experience is with Mulia, a plump woman, who teaches him the art of love. After his experience with her, he gains confidence and tries to prove his masculinity with other women. The next one is Samyukta, his cousin, who is of his age. Then, he goes to different prostitutes and gains victory over them. Finally, he meets Roop Singh's mother who drains him out. Now he is crestfallen. He says,

> She was some kind of a vampire, a succubus—I swear to it—and she was determined to drain me of my last ounce of manhood.[41]

He wants to escape from her but she does not leave him. He gets release from her with the help of her younger son. After returning home, he fails with Mulia and Samyukta and later on with Shankhini. Frustrated with his weakness, he leaves home and becomes a recluse. Here, in the cave, he gets solace. He says:

> And yet this weed which grows all about me, has made life tolerable. It has so solaced me that in my fantasies I can experience all those sensual pleasures without my miserable body having to do anything! Surely that's an achievement—surely that's victory for mind over matter![42]

But the narrator does not agree with him and refutes the recluse:

> I wouldn't call it that. If it's the plant that brings you mental ease, that makes it a victory of matter over mind. Surely the only victory comes when mind is free.[43]

The recluse confesses his helplessness. He says that he has been a sensualist and sought sensual pleasure in the world. He received a gift from the Divine but misused it. He destroyed the gift by misusing it. Since he cannot retrieve it, he has renounced the world and taken shelter in that lonely cave.

The narrator replies him befittingly:

> But the world isn't exclusively a place for the pursuit of sensual pleasure.[44]

Before his departure, the narrator asks the address of the hill woman who sucked all his strength. The recluse says that it will be something dangerous for the narrator as he may lose his manhood. But the narrator does not agree with him.

> No. I wish to regain it. Or rather. I wish to discover it. And only a woman who can give so much of herself can revive true passion in a man.[45]

The recluse replies that the narrator is wrong in his opinion. A woman of great passion can only diminish a man. The narrator refutes him by giving the reason that he was in love with his ego and too much concerned with his self-esteem. As a result of his egoism he lost everything. After refuting him the narrator leaves the cave. The novella ends with these lines:

> And I leave him in the cave with his cold thoughts, and the cold ashes of his dead fire, and the cold corpse he still inhabits.
>
> I leave my dead self in the cave and continue my search for the perfect stranger in the night.

The end is enigmatic and appears rather forced. Here, we come to know that the recluse is the other self of the narrator who defeats it, leaves it cold and goes in search of a new life.

The novella, as said earlier, begins with a promise but collapses in the middle. It is only towards the end that it revives with a flicker. The great problem with Ruskin Bond here is that his fantasy is not the displacement of reality. Every writer fantasies but there is some reality at the base. He or she changes the names of people and places and makes the incidents more interesting by his or her art of what Viktor Shklovsky has named defamiliarisation. The weakness of Bond is that he has reversed the process. What is unreal he has tried to make real. The quotation in the beginning is a kind of warning and it advises the people to refrain from lust and sensuality. The scholars in the past exhorted people to refrain from woman and wealth (Kamini and Kanchan). Bond has failed to understand the spirit of the Sanskrit saying and interpreted it too literally. Secondly, he has not been able to make the hill woman, Roop Singh's mother, a mysterious figure. The relationship between the recluse and the hill woman appears to be very-very unreal and so are all his experiences.

Finally, the novella fails as a piece of literature. It is only a potboiler. The last page is like a patch of silver electroplating.

NOTES

1. *Collected Fiction*, 7.
2. *Ibid.*, 13.
3. *Ibid.*, 310.
4. *Rain in the Mountains* (Delhi: Penguin, 1993), 240.
5. *Scenes from a Writer's Life*, 151-52.
6. *Ibid.*, 153.
7. *Rain in Mountains*, 240-41.
8. *Ibid.*, 41.
9. *Ibid.*, 57.
10. *Ruskin Bond: Complete Fiction*, 44.
11. *Ibid.*, 46.
12. *Ibid.*, 47.
13. *Ibid.*, 48.

14. *Rain in the Mountains*, 245.
15. B.S. Naikar, "The Paradox of Love" in Love is a Sad Song, *The Creative Contours of Ruskin Bond*, ed. P.K. Singh, 96.
16. *Ruskin Bond: Collected Fiction*, 187.
17. *Ibid.*, 190.
18. *Idem.*, 190.
19. *Ibid.*, 189.
20. *Ibid.*, 193.
21. *Ibid.*, 194.
22. *Ibid.*, 213.
23. *Ibid.*, 215.
24. *Ibid.*, 248.
25. Murari Prasad, "Time Capsule: A study of Time Stops at Shamli and Other Stories", *The Creative Contours of Ruskin Bond*, ed. P.K. Singh, 111.
26. *Ruskin Bond: Complete Fiction*, 819-20.
27. *Ibid.*, 268-69.
28. *Ibid.*, 256.
29. *Ibid.*, 257-58.
30. *Ibid.*, 265.
31. *Ibid.*, 267.
32. *Ibid.*, 271.
33. *Ibid.*, 280.
34. *Ibid.*, 101.
35. *Idem.*, 101.
36. *Idem.*, 102.
37. *Ibid.*, 102.
38. *Idem.*, 102.
39. *Idem.*
40. *Collected Fiction*, 901.
41. *Ibid.*, 938.
42. *Ibid.*, 945.
43. *Ibid.*, 946.
44. *Ibid.*
45. *Idem.*

7

Technique and Art of Narration

Ruskin Bond is traditional in technique and art of narration. He does not follow avant-garde novelists and short-story writers of our time and keeps himself aloof from modernism and postmodernism. He follows the line of Dickens, Kipling, Jack London and Hugh Walpole. He counts the authors whom he read and who influenced him greatly. The passage is rather long:

> I owe a lot to that school library, and to whatever left me in complete charge of it, for I had the keys and could go there at odd hours, ostensibly to catalogue the books but in reality to pore through them and become familiar with both the illustrations and the unfamiliar. In stolen moments over a period of three years, I read all the novels of Dickens, Stevenson, Jack London, Hugh Walpole, J.B. Priestley, the Bronte's (in no particular order) the complete plays of J.M. Barrie, Bernard Shaw, A.A. Milne, Somerset Maugham and Ben Travers, and the essays—and it was a great time for essayist—of A.G. Gardiner (*Alpha of the Plough*) Robert Lynd, Priestley again, Belloe, Chesterton and many others. And then, of course, there were the humorous writers—Mark Twain, Thurber, Wodehouse, Stephen Leacock, Jerome K. Jerome, W.W. Jacobs, Barry Pain, H.G. Wells (in his shorter works), Damon Runyon—I lapped them all up. My favourite humorous book, then and now, is *The Diary of a Nobody* by George and William Grossmith; it never fails to make me laugh, even

though I must have read it over ten times. Five years ago, it cured me of a peptic ulcer.[1]

These facts emerge from this passage:

1. Bond wanted to be a writer.
2. He read the authors of the Victorian age in his formative years.
3. All the authors in his list have written in the traditional way.
4. There is a marked inclination in Bond to wit and humour.

The writers whom he read at the young age of thirteen to sixteen years influenced his technique of novel writing and narration of stories. We find that he does not mention Flaubert, Dostoevsky, Maupassant, Conrad, Lawrence, Joyce, Proust and Virginia Woolf. Even the recent writers are not included in the list. What is his technique then?

Before analysing his technique, it is pertinent to have a look at the technique of the eighteenth and nineteenth century novelists. Henry Fielding called *Tom Jones* "a comic epic in prose". Here the words "epic", "comic" and "prose" are significant. For Fielding the novel is the prose form of the epic. It is as large and comprehensive in structure as the epic. The first difference between the two is that whereas the epic is in verse, the novel is in prose. The second is that the epic is serious but the novel, at least *Tom Jones,* is comic. It is not tragic. Aldous Huxley in his famous essay "Tragedy and the Whole Truth" considers Homer's *Odyssey* an epic of the whole truth where all the truths of life—comic and tragic—are present. He says that all modern novels are the novels of whole truth:

> A book can be written in terms of pure phantasy and yet, by implication, tell the whole Truth. Of all the important works of contemporary literature not one is a pure tragedy. There is no contemporary writer of significance who does not prefer to state or imply the whole Truth. However different one from another in style, in ethical, philosophical and artistic intention, in the scales of values accepted,

> contemporary writers have this in common, that they are interested in the whole Truth. Proust, D.H. Lawrence, André Gide, Kafka, Hemingway—here are five obviously significant and important contemporary writers. Five authors as remarkably unlike one another as they could well be. They are at one only in this, that none of them has written a pure tragedy, that all are concerned with the whole Truth.[2]

The purpose of quoting this passage is to prove that Ruskin Bond's novels and short-stories are the fiction of the whole truth and that, even when he has tried to be experimental, say in *Love is a Sad Song,* he has depicted life in all its details, not the tragic aspect only. In short Bond is basically traditional in his technique but modern or contemporary in the depiction of life around him.

The traditional novelist follows the old Aristotelian principle of structure and the imposition of form on the content. The elements or components of the traditional novel are: plot, character, art of narration and style. The first two shall be discussed in the first section of this chapter and the last two in the second.

I

Plot Construction—Plot is not a story; it is much more than that. E.M. Forster in his famous book *Aspects of the Novel* makes distinction between a story and a plot. He says that the difference between the two is that the former is a sequence of events whereas the latter is a *logical* sequence of events. "A king died; A queen died," is a story but "A king died and the queen died out of grief" is a plot.[3] The first does not show any logical relations between the two events but in the second the reason of the queen's death is present. It follows then that a novel or a short story must have a logical sequence of events. Aristotle, father of Western literary criticism, goes much beyond E.M. Forster. According to him the plot includes all the speeches, utterances and figures of speech. Besides literary devices and characters have their existence in the system of the plot.

The plot must be a whole: it means it must have a beginning, a middle and an end. Besides, it should be of a certain magnitude for being beautiful. Then all the parts of the text must be of a certain size in relation to the plot. The plot should have unity of action. Seen from this point of view Bond's plot construction is masterly. As all his novels are short in length, he organizes the events in a masterly way. No part of his novels is irrelevant or superfluous. All the events are closely linked and all characters too.

Bond begins his novels with a description of the surroundings. The purpose is to build the atmosphere. After that, in the manner of Sir Walter Scott and Thomas Hardy, he introduces the main character but does not name him. *The Room on the Roof* begins thus:

> The light spring rain rode on the wind, into the trees, down the road; it brought an exhilarating freshness to the air, a smell of earth, a scent of flowers; it brought a smile to the eyes of the boy on the road.
>
> The long road wound round the hills, rose and fell and twisted down to Dehra; the road came from the mountains and passed through the jungle and valley and, after passing through Dehra, ended somewhere in the bazaar. But just where it ended no one knew, for the bazaar was a baffling place, where roads were easily lost.
>
> The boy was three miles out of Dehra. The further he could get from Dehra, the happier he was likely to be. Just now he was only three miles out of Dehra, so he was not very happy; and, what was worse, he was walking homewards.[4]

Right from the beginning, the two worlds are contrasted: the free world of the adolescent and the oppressive home ruled by the cruel guardian. The boy is happy in the company of nature but when he nears home, he feels sad. This is typical of Bond that the opening pages of his novels and short stories create an atmosphere which is sustained throughout.

Secondly, he uses the technique of defamiliarization. The boy's name is not given in the beginning. It is only towards the end of the chapter we come to know that his name is Rusty. Viktor Shklovsky, a great Russian critic and one of the leaders of Russian Formalism, coined the term defamiliarization and said that it is the chief characteristic of literary writing:

> The technique of art is to make objects "unfamiliar", to make forms difficult, to increase the difficulty and length of perception because the process of perception is an aesthetic end in itself and must be prolonged. *Art is a way of experiencing the artfulness of an object; the object is not important.*[5] (Italics mine)

David Lodge gives the alternate translation of the italicised sentence:

> The translation of this crucial and often quoted sentence by Lemon and Reis has been criticized by Robert Scholes, who offers his own version: "In art, it is our experience of the process of construction that counts, not the finished product."[6] (*Structuralism in Literature,* 1947, p. 84)

We are not concerned with the controversy between the translators; what is important for us is the word "unfamiliar". While reading a literary text or viewing a work of art, we are surprised by the strangeness, the way a work of art is done. What is quotidian reality becomes something fresh and strange.

Shklovsky explains and illustrates the process of making things unfamiliar in the same essay and analyses a few passages from Leo Tolstoy. One of the passages is quoted:

> Tolstoy makes the familiar seem strange by not naming the familiar object. He describes an object as if he were seeing it for the first time, an event as if it were happening for the first time. In describing something he avoids the accepted names of its parts and instead names corresponding parts of other objects. For example, in "Shame" Tolstoy *defamiliarises* the idea of flogging in this way....[7]

Bond defamiliarises the day-to-day happening by mystifying it, by not naming it or by giving a fictitious name, which, in fact, does not exist. Here, the total scene is described but the boy's name is not given, nor is he introduced in the first or second paragraph; slowly and slowly he is revealed and only towards the end we are able to see him in full.

This technique of *defamiliarization* or *bestrangement* is employed in all his novels, except *A Flight of Pigeons* and a few short stories. *Vagrants in the Valley* begins:

> On the road to Dehra a boy played on a flute as he drove his flock of sheep down the road. He was barefoot and his clothes were old. A faded red shawl was thrown across his shoulders. It was December and the sun was up, pouring into the banyan tree at the side of the road where two boys were sitting on the great tree's gnarled, protruding roots.[8]

We never know who the flute playing boy is. But the two boys resting under the tree are also made unfamiliar. It is only in the fifth paragraph we come to know that one is Rusty and, a little later, the other is Kishen. Gradually, their identity emerges. Kishen's mention of Somi's name reminds us that Rusty is the Rusty of *The Room on the Roof* and Kishen is Kishen, Mrs. Kapoor's son. We understand with a pleasant surprise that the novel is a sequel of *The Room on the Roof*.

This technique of making familiar things unfamiliar is most manifest in the short story *Time Stops at Shamli* and the novella *The Sensualist*. The opening paragraph of the story is already quoted. What is most significant is that the whole atmosphere of the story and the people are strange and finally the appearance of Sushila takes us by surprise. Similarly the first two pages of the novella, *The Sensualist,* lead us through the strange and mysterious boulders and rocks in the hills. The traveller does not meet any human beings on the way. Finally, he reaches the top of the hill and sees something strange and unfamiliar:

> There is someone squatting, crouching at the entrance to the cave. As the sun is in my eyes, I cannot be sure if the creature is human or animal. It doesn't move. It is black and almost formless.[9]

Secondly, the story moves chronologically. The novel that attained its maturity in the eighteenth century in the hands of Henry Fielding had plots that had chronological development.

The reader watched the growth of the protagonist in the numbers of years. Sometimes, the author narrated the past of characters or the events that had occurred before the hero's or heroine's birth. This method of plot construction continued till the end of the nineteenth century. It was only in the twentieth century that the novelists set aside the traditional technique of plot-construction. Marcel Proust, James Joyce and Virginia Woolf did not follow the time sequence in their novels. Present, past and future merged together. The novelists who came after them did not break completely with the tradition but followed these innovators largely.

Bond is least influenced by the stream-of-conscious technique. He is like Dickens, P.G. Wodehouse and Rudyard Kipling. We watch the growth of Rusty and his friends. The novel is rather episodic, though the chapters are not titled. But in the *Vagrants in the Valley* each chapter is titled and so is the case with *A Flight of Pigeons*. *Delhi is Not Far* appears to be a psychological novel in the beginning:

> My balcony is my window on the world.
>
> The room has one window, a square hole in the wall crossed by three iron bars.
>
> The view from it is a restricted one. If I crane my neck sideways and put my nose to the bars, I can see the extremeties of the building; below, a narrow courtyard where children—the children of all classes of people—play together. It is only when they are older that they become conscious of the barrier of class and caste.[10]

This mood of reflection continues throughout the first chapter. In fact, it reads like an autobiographical novel.

A Flight of Pigeons is in the form of diary and hence its appeal is direct. The author begins it in the most prosaic words but when Ruth comes to the scene the whole scenario changes. The difference between history and reminiscence is wide. A historian is objective, dry, almost emotionless. Besides, he is critical occasionally and in support of his arguments he presents facts. The diarist is, on the other hand, emotional and perceptive. The reason is that all the events and people described affect his or her life. Ruth's diary binds the reader with her and her mother. We, having great sympathy for the 1857 war, forget that they are aliens, members of the society that wrongly ruled us. We consciously or unconsciously wish for their safety. The defeat of the Indian revolutionaries is painful and frustrating for us, yet we feel relief when we see Ruth and her family return home safely.

Finally, Bond builds the plots of his novels slowly and we reach the climax only towards the end. He has not followed the old tradition of exposition, complication, climax, anti-climax and conclusion. Climax and conclusion are almost blended and there is no anti-climax. The exposition is long. First the atmosphere is built. In *The Room on the Roof,* complication comes much later. It is only after the quarrel between Mr. Harrison and Rusty that complication begins. This complication continues for a long time. One episode leads to the other. The climax comes when Mrs. Kapoor dies in the car accident and Kishen is asked to go to his aunt. But soon, the conclusion follows. Kishen and Rusty are united again and return to Dehra.

Bond has kept his plots deliberately simple. If we compare his novels with those of Forster or Greene, we find that the more famous novelists always have a sub plot. But Bond's novels have only one plot. The story revolves round one or two characters; there are no digressions. As a result of this, his novels are short, well-knit and compact. There is no character, no paragraph, nor any page that can be torn away without affecting the plot.

Characterisation—Characters are usually divided into simple and complex or flat and round.[11] Simple or flat characters remain the same throughout the novel but complex or round characters change. A good novelist creates both kinds of characters. A great novelist has a good number of characters in her or his novels. Tolstoy, Dostoevsky, Gorky, George Eliot, Charles Dickens, Henry James, D.H. Lawrence and Prem Chand have a variety of characters in their novels. The characters are mostly complex and a few simple.

The second aspect of characterisation is the psychological insight. Dickens and Chaucer are more concerned with the outward appearance and behaviour of their characters. Dickens describes Miss Trotwood, Mr. Bounderby, Uriah Heep, David Copperfield, Joe Gargery, Pirrip and other characters in terms of their physical appearance. The characters act as they appear to be. We easily anticipate how they will act in a particular situation. George Eliot, Tolstoy and Dostoevsky, on the hand, go deep into the psychology of their characters. Their characters think and feel at the same time. In *War and Peace* Prince Andre feels and thinks deeply at the death of Little Princess and so does he at the time of his own death. Count Pierre when he finds his wife faithless and injures her lover in a duel, he begins to think emotionally. He realises that his wife has every right to live her own life and also that her lover should not be considered a bad man. He goes to the major's house, sees him and his old mother and helps them. Similarly, there is a lot of psychological insight in *Brothers Karmazov* and *Crime and Punishment*. George Eliot is an expert in the psychological analysis of her characters. Dorothea's psyche is admirably explored in *Middlemarch*.

Bond has created both flat and round characters. The major characters are round or complex and the minor characters flat or simple in his novels.

Rusty, Mrs. Kapoor, Kishen, Kamla, Javed, Mrs. Labadoor and Sushila are complex characters. The other characters play a minor role.

Rusty, of course, is the most complex and most important characters. He is delineated in full. We learn about his parentage, his relatives, his upbringing, his revolt, his mixing with the Indian adolescents of his age and finally his search for identity and struggle for the desired goal. His physical appearance is described in detail:

> He was a pale boy, with blue-grey eyes and fair hair; his face was rough and marked, and the lower lip hung loose and heavy. He had his hands in his pockets and his head down, which was the way he always walked, and which gave him a deceptively tired appearance. He was a lazy but not a tired person.[12]

Bond takes pain in describing his mental workings. When he is beaten badly by his guardian and when he is unable to bear the injustice and pain, he retaliates. As he is young and strong, he hits Mr. Harrison hard. His triumph over the tyrant guardian gives him a new kind of feeling. Bond aptly describes his mental process:

> The look of alarm on Mr. Harrison's face gave Rusty greater courage. Before the man could recover his feet and his balance, Rusty gripped him by the collar and pushed him backwards, until they both fell over on to the floor. With one hand still twisting the collar, the boy slapped his guardian's face. Mad with the pain in his own face, Rusty hit the man again and again, wildly and awkwardly, but with the giddy thrill of knowing he could do it; he was a child no longer, he was nearly seventeen, he was a man. He could inflict pain, that was a wonderful discovery; there was a power in his body—a devil or a god—and he gained confidence in his power; and he was a man![13]

This is his transformation from a child into a young man. Similarly, his feelings after Mrs. Kapoor's death in car accident, is of a post-adolescent:

> Meena is dead, he told himself, Meena is dead. If there is a god, then God will look after her; if God is Love, then my love will be with her. She loved me. I can see her so clearly, her face speckled with sun and shadow when we kissed in the forest, the black waterfall of hair, her tired eyes, her feet like jade in the lamplight, she loved me, she was mine....
>
> Rusty was overcome by a feeling of impotence and futility, and of unimportance of life. Every moment, he told himself, every moment someone is born and someone dies, you can count them one, two, three, a birth and a death for every moment.... What is this one life in the whole pattern of life, what is this one death but a passing of time....[14]

Rusty is the fully grown character in *The Room on the Roof, Vagrants in the Valley* and *Delhi is Not Far.* The other male characters are all adolescents, barring Mr. Kapoor, Mr. Harrison, Mr. Pettigrew and the American who are adults.

Bond has delineated the adolescents in the most perfect manner. Chhotu and Kishen, who have not reached their teenage, are funny, pucky and sunny at the same time. They behave as a child does. Somi, Ranbir, Devinder, Sudheer and Suri are adolescents. Somi is energetic and vivacious as a growing adolescent should be. He is helpful and generous to Rusty. He is his perfect friend. Ranbir is equally helpful though he is not like Somi. Devinder and Sudheer are quite different. Sudheer, the loafer, is certainly a spoiled adolescent by our standard but he is not a bad man altogether. He belongs to the underworld as Kishen had been after his mother's death and it was only his reunion with Rusty that saved his future career. Sudheer, though educated does not make use of his learning in constructive works. He has connection with two prostitutes—Mrinalini and Hastini. He cheats people, but only the well-off not the destitutes like Rusty and Devinder. He helps Rusty with money and accompanies him to the hills.

Devinder studies and sells combs and buttons. He is an example of the self-made boys. His twin or clone is the thin, long-limbed and bony boy Suraj. An epilectic, he too, reads in a school and is preparing for the test or examination to qualify for admission into a college and scholarship. Devinder is less developed in *Vagrants in the Valley* but Suraj is fully depicted. He lives with Rusty (Rusty's name is not mentioned anywhere in *Delhi is Not Far*) and is largely dependent on him. In fact, Rusty is his friend, philosopher and guide. Just as Kishen under the guidance of Rusty becomes a healthy adolescent, Suraj also gains confidence and passes the examination with flying colours. Once an orphan (he missed his parents at the station while fleeing from Pakistan) and epilectic, he is towards the end of the novel, a healthy young man with an optimistic outlook.

All the male adolescents in Bond's novels are poverty-stricken people. The only exceptions are Somi and Ranbir. Kishen, too becomes a destitute after his mother's death. They live in a wretched condition and earn money by selling combs and buttons, cheating the people and in the case of Rusty by writing stories for magazines. This world is quite different from the middle-class world. The characters act more instinctively than rationally. Their fundamental problem is how to eat and live and find a place in this world where they are on the margin. Yet they are all sunny. They enjoy life. Poverty is there, hunger is there and the future is bleak but they are all optimistic.

When we come to the female characters, we find that Ruth is the only adolescent in Bond's novels; the rest are all fully grown up adults. Mrinalini, Hastini and Kamla, the three prostitutes, have crossed the age of adolescence.

Meena Kapoor is the frustrated housewife. Married at the young age of thirteen to the aged Kapoor, she is deprived of love when she enters her thirties. Her estrangement with her indolent husband impels her to look the other way. When Rusty sees her and is enamoured with her, she falls in love with him. Both, despite the difference in age, become lovers. It is a bit puzzling for us that a mother of a twelve years son can fall in love with a seventeen years adolescent. The car accident is inevitable in the development of the plot as such a love cannot be sustained for a long time.

Mrinalini and Hastini are professional sex-workers. Here, Bond successfully depicts the private life of prostitutes. The way they behave with Sudheer leads us to realize the truth that love, affection and sex are different things. A prostitute sleeps with a customer for money. It is only a touch and go affair. But in their private life, they are different people. They too want to love and be loved.

Kamla is another prostitute. Married to a villager she becomes a sex worker and lives in a dormitory owned by Seth Govind Ram. Her relation with the narrator in *Delhi is Not Far* is friendly. She sleeps with him and also, on his advice, with Suraj. She does not go to Delhi with the narrator as she has her home and family.

The other important character is Sushila. The narrator saw her when she was nine or ten years old and fell in love with her when she reached sixteen but could not marry her because of the age difference and other reasons, the most important being his economic instability. Later on, he meets Sushila after her marriage to a well-to-do aged man. Sushila still loves him but will not go with him.

Madhu is the other female character who dies at the young age of thirteen or fourteen. Supported and educated by the narrator, she begins to love him. There is a great age difference but love is not bound by the norms of society. She dies because she is asked to study in a school far away from the narrator. Her dying words reveal her heart that she wanted to be his wife.

If we look at all these female characters—Meena, Kamla, Sushila and Madhu—we find that there is age difference. Meena and Kamla, both married, are older than the narrator and Sushila and Madhu are much younger. Secondly, there is extra-marital relationship in all cases except that of Madhu.

This age difference persists in *A Flight of Pigeons* where Javed Khan wants to marry Ruth, a girl of thirteen. Why is it that Bond shows love between a mature man and a thirteen year old girl? Why is it a girl, only thirteen, is attracted to an adult. At the end of *A Flight of Pigeons,* Ruth reflects:

> He (Javed Khan) was very wild and muddle headed, and often cruel, but he was also very handsome and gallant, and there was in him a streak of nobility which he did his best to conceal. But perhaps I really admire him because he thought I was beautiful.[15]

The answer is difficult. Perhaps, Bond can better explain the reason.

The characters in *A Flight of Pigeons* are fully drawn, especially, Mariam, Javed Khan, Lala Ramjimal, Kothiwali and Qamran. Mariam is heroic. She faces her husband's tragic death stoically and is the brave pilot of the drifting ship of her family. Javed Khan, despite his arrogance and rowdyism is noble and a true follower of Islam. Kothiwali and Qamran are typical Muslim women of the time.

Bond's World—If we ignore the world of Bond's novels and short stories, we will not be able to understand his technique fully and also the reasons why characters act in a special way. In his famous book *Aspects of the Novel* E.M. Forster writes:

> The novelist...has a very mixed lot of ingredients to handle...he prefers to tell his story about human beings; he takes over the life by values as well as the life in time. The characters arrive when evoked, but full of the spirit of mutiny. For they have these numerous parallels with people like ourselves, they try to live their own lives and are often engaged in treason against the main scheme of the book. They 'run away', they 'get out of hand'; *they are creations inside a creation....*[16] (Italics mine)

Here Forster makes it amply clear that characters act in a world created by the novelist: "they are creations inside a creation". Therefore it is imperative for us to examine the kind of the world Bond has created in his novels and short stories.

The fictional world of Bond is rather limited and represents the area near the Siwalik hills in northern India. The flora and fauna are sub-Himalayan. The trees are oak, cherry, deodar, pine, litchi, mango and pipal. The flowers are chrysanthemum, dahlia, marigold, flox, hollyhock and gulmohar. The people are simple and unambitious. In fact, this world is quite different from the world of India's plains. The bazaar is ordinary and nowhere Bond gives a description of big shops of readymade garments and jewellery.

The people who inhabit this world are poor by our standards. The only rich people are Seth Govind Ram, Mr. Kapoor and Mrs. Bhushan. Somi and Ranbir come from the middle class. Rusty, Suraj, Devinder, Sudheer, Deep Chand, Kamla, Mrinalini, Hastini, Goonga, Pitambar and Ganpat are people living below the poverty line. One quality of the poor people is that they are honest and do not think of cheating their own people. Secondly, they help one another in critical periods. For people like Rusty even twenty rupees is a large sum but Sudheer, the Lafunga, helps him with fifteen rupees. The kind of meal they take is rather cheap.

Naturally, the talk and action of the people is generally personal. They are least concerned with the administration or politics of their town. Although they are doubled with economic burden, they do not complain and remain satisfied with what they get. The only ambitious character is Rusty who aspires to be an eminent writer. The characters in *A Flight of Pigeons* too are more interested in their local, personal and family affairs. The female characters in this novel are interested in their household affairs and children. They are all simple people.

People tell and listen to ghost stories. Ganpat tells the story of Bippin, the ghost who lives in a pipal tree and who gives him a lot of money on the condition he would sleep with him. When Ganpat breaks the promise, Bippin hits him hard on the back with the result that he is doubled up. It is not that only the Hindus believe in the existence of ghosts but Muslims and Christians too. Mariam tells the story of a jinn and all people believe that her story is true.

The fictional world of Bond is like that of Jane Austen. Jane Austen remained confined to the middle class families of the country area of England in the eighteenth century. Ruskin remains confined to the middle and lower classes of Garhwal.

II

Ruskin Bond is one of the finest story-tellers in Indian fiction. Right from the beginning to the end, our attention is seldom lax. We go on reading his short-stories till we have finished them. Often he follows the traditional mixed method. Novelists in the eighteenth century adopted the method of the author as an omniscient. In other words, they narrated the story in their own words as if they were present everywhere. Henry Fielding and Daniel Defoe largely followed this method of narration. The other method of narration was the autobiographical method. Here the narrator was not the author but the main character who told the story of his or her life. The third was the epistolary method. Different characters wrote letters and narrated the events and their thought-processes to other characters. The autobiographical and epistolary methods of narration gave novelists greater freedom to present a variety of characters and make them complex. Jane Austen combined these three methods of narration and added dialogues to make certain situations dramatic and more lively. The famous novel, *Pride and Prejudice,* after preliminary remarks has a dramatic beginning. The whole situation becomes lively when Mr. and Mrs. Bennet begin to talk and Mrs. Bennet expresses her concern for her daughter's marriage.

Bond has followed Sir Walter Scott, Jane Austen, Charles Dickens and Rudyard Kipling. He has deliberately avoided the experimentalists or avant-garde novelists like James Joyce and Virginia Woolf. However, he has made use of the technique of narration of modern novelists like Greene and Golding and Vladimir Nabokov.

His art of narration can be best analysed in terms of narratology. Narratology is a specialised branch of structuralist criticism which analyses and evaluates a literary work as a linguistic structure. David Lodge has summarised the basic concepts of narratology in his famous book *Working with Structuralism.*[17]

First, a distinction is made between *fabula* and *sjuzet. Fabula* is the raw material (an event or experience) and *sjuzet* is the product of the organized events or experiences. The art of narration lies in the way the different events and experiences are organized.

How does a writer organize the sjuzet? There are two forces that shape his skill: the past conventions and his own acumen. Narratology examines an author's art of narration on the following principles.

(a) The progress of a story is dialectical, not circular. There is the initiating action and then the counter action and finally the terminating event which reconciles the previous conflicting actions and events.

This principle of narration can be compared to I.A. Richard's notion of synaesthesis. Richards in his *Principles of Literary Criticism* says that a good poem arouses conflicting emotions which are synthesised at the end and the reader experiences the harmony of feelings and experiences.

(b) Secondly, there are actants and functions. An actant can have only one function or more than one function. Likewise a function can have one actant or more than one actant. Since every text is a kind of narration, and the authorial voice is continuously discernible, the technique of narratology is applied to establish the relationship between the actants and the functions and the catalysers.

(c) Thirdly, an author makes certain stylistic choices (symbolism, irony, humour, wit and literary tropes) to make his narration literary and appealing to the reader's imagination. It is also that the author's intention is to arouse certain kind of emotion in the reader. Therefore, a study of style is a part of narratology.

(d) Finally, the title is of utmost significance. In the words of Roland Barthes:

> ...the function of the title is to mark the beginning of the text, that is, to constitute the text as a commodity. Every title thus has several simultaneous meanings, including at least these two: (i) what it says is linked to the contingency of what follows it; (ii) the announcement itself that a piece of literature (which means, in fact, a piece of commodity) is going to follow; in other words, the title always has a double function; enunciating and deictic.[18]

The term deictic is an adjective and it means "of or denoting a word or expression whose meaning is dependent on the context in which it is used." A little later, he writes on the same page that the title has an aperitive function; it whets the reader's appetite.

We shall analyse Bond's art of narration in the light of the points discussed above.

First, Bond's titles have both initiating and deictic functions. The titles of the short stories "Night Train at Deoli", "Love is a Sad Song", "The Woman on the Platform", "Time Stops at Shamli" and of the novels *The Room on the Roof, Vagrants in the Valley, Delhi is Not Far, A Flight of Pigeons* and *The Sensualist* whet our appetite. We begin to wonder at these strange and colourful titles. Our curiosity is aroused and we read the text with great interest. Thus the next function begins. We want to know what the title means. Since the function is deictic, the meaning can be found in the context which is the text itself. After reading the short story "Night Train at Deoli", we come to know why the author has chosen the title. So is the case with the other titles.

Secondly, the progress of narration is always dialectical. In "Night Train at Deoli", there is a contrast between the world of the railway of which the narrator is a part and the world beyond the railway walls. The link between the two is the girl who sells baskets. The narrator establishes friendliness with the linking chain, the basket seller, but once that chain is broken (the girl is not seen on the platform), the other world remains only a hope. "Time Stops at Shamli" is a continuation of the previous story. This time the narrator goes beyond the railway walls, meets Sushila and the mystery is resolved. But the story ends in a different way. The two worlds meet to be separated again. Both worlds meander, sometimes together and sometimes apart.

Since the novels have a larger number of characters, there is polyphony of voices of actants who function differently. At first there are Rusty and Harrison. Harrison initiates the action of restricting the adolescent Rusty. Rusty is prohibited from crossing the world of the civil lines which represents the middle class white people and the upper class Indian people. Rusty's action is to break this boundary line and go to the free world of the hills and of the common people symbolised by the bazaar. The story develops on the dialectics of the jail life dominated by Harrison and Rusty's action of liberation. The result is obvious: the old yields to the new.

Now the dialectics is on another plane which is the problem of existence. An orphan adolescent without any legacy or support has to struggle for his livelihood and fulfil his aspiration to become an established writer. Our curiosity is sustained throughout till we reach the end of the novel.

In *Vagrants in the Valley*, Rusty's problems continue. This time he is not alone; he has the burden of Kishen. The dialectics continues: Rusty's continuous effort to get a job for his livelihood and the hostile world before him. His approaches to Mr. Pettigrew and his aunt with the hookah living in the interiors of the hills do not prove to be of great help in the beginning. It is Sudheer, the Lafunga, who helps him. Rusty's journey and meeting with different kinds of people move dialectically. The different actions, heterogeneous and conflicting, strengthen Rusty and at last, he finds the true path. The books that Rusty gets from his aunt and Pettigrew's assessment of their value help Rusty to fulfil his ambition of going to England and learn the trade of writing.

The Sensualist presents the dialectics of the two actants and their functions in the most direct and sharpest way. There is the young narrator who labours hard to cross the ascending hill to go to Kapila, a village on the bank of a stream. He has lost his path and is now in an area quite unknown to him, an area of small grass and dry rocks and small caves. At last he comes to a place where there is a recluse.

The recluse is the sensualist. He has had a lustful life. He tells the narrator that he was proud that he could win any woman. He was really a victorious man. But one day he finds that all his vigour is spent. He renounces the physical world. He advises the narrator to follow his example and accept the fact that mind has superiority over body. The narrator does not agree; he believes in the balance of the two. He says:

> That is because you were in love with your ego, you were too concerned about your self-esteem. You took the love but not spurned the lover. And so you had to lose both. I hope to find them yet....[19]

The third feature of Bond's art of narration is the use of symbols. A symbol is a concrete word which refers to or represents an abstract idea. For example, Byzantium is a concrete word and it represents Yeats's idea of unity of culture in the poem "Sailing to Byzantium" and the long legged bird is the symbol of longevity in "Lapis Lazuli". A symbol is a simple word that occurs a number of times in an author's work and with each occurrence it grows richer in meaning. "The room" on the top of the roof of Mrs. Kapoor's house is an ordinary room in the beginning but later on it stands for the author's world. It is also a watch tower from where, he can see the go of the world. It is a place of his imaginative creativity. Its full significance is realised in *Delhi is Not Far*: "My balcony is my window on the world." In the first three novels, the room has its own role to play like Edgan Heath in Hardy's *The Return of the Native*.

The bazaar is the other symbol in *The Room on the Roof*. It stands for the common people and their world. It is a prohibited place for the white people and rich people like Mr. Kapoor. Rusty and Kishen are not allowed to go there. But it has its own life and vivacity. The civil lines is sickly and lifeless. In contrast, the bazaar is full of life and activity. It is the ideal place for the adolescents where they enjoy untrammelled freedom.

The rainy season is the third important symbol. It stands for life regenerating force. In India, the rainy season is eagerly awaited. The land is parched and the heat wave dries even the blood of the body. The arrival of dark clouds and the cool gust of wind refreshes everybody. Rusty feels regenerated when the rainy season comes. Not only he, but also all the people of the town rejoice. We see Rusty in Chapter Nineteen of *The Room on the Roof*. He is sad after the death of Meena Kapoor and departure of Kishen. Days pass by and so does the summer season. The rainy season arrives. The first showers wash away Rusty's sadness:

> The rain was more intoxicating than the alcohol, and it was with difficulty that he restrained himself from shouting and dancing in mad abandon. The force and freshness of the rain brought tremendous relief, washed away the stagnation that had been settling on him, poisoning mind and body.[20]

In all his novels and stories, rains have an invigorating and regenerating effect. They are described in detail and with all vividness.

The fourth symbol, stream, is closely related to rain. According to myth critics water is the symbol of the source of life. In the novels of Bond, stream is the great source of joy for the adolescents. They drink water and swim in the cool and refreshing water. In the *Vagrants in the Valley* Rusty walks a long distance to see a particular river. When he is almost exhausted he hears the sound of a river and then sees the river. The sight puts new life in him:

> Far down in the valley, the river stretched and opened into broad, beautiful motion, and Rusty gasped and began to run. He slipped and stumbled but still he ran. Then he was ankle-deep in the cold mountain water.
>
> All the water was blue and white and wonderful.[21]

Finally, humour is one of the most important characteristics of Bond's art of narration. Without humour, a narration becomes dull and insipid. Shakespeare introduced the porter scene in *Macbeth* just before Duncan's murder. Shakespeare's use of humour in his great tragedies is masterly. Bond uses humour to enliven his narration. His humour is pure and innocent. We laugh without malice. Mrs. Bhushan, a character in *Vagrants in the Valley,* comes to take Kishen her home. Kishen wants to take Rusty with him. Mrs. Bhushan, a robust and highly assertive woman, asks him to come alone into her car. Then she drives speedily. The authorial comment is full of humour:

> And she trod on the accelerator with such ferocity that a lame beggar, who had been dawdling in the middle of the road, suddenly regained the use of both legs and sprang nimbly on to the pavement.[22]

Similarly the publisher's advice to the narrator, an emerging creative writer, is full of humour with an ironical undertone:

> (Students) want to get...degrees the easy way without reading too many books or attending more than half a dozen lectures.... Why should they wade through five volumes of political history when they can get a dozen model answer-papers?[23]

The authorial comment on the character of the business man Seth Govind reveals the hidden opportunism of the Seth in particular and his class in general.

> Seth Govind Ram is a prominent member of the municipality. Publicly, he is a staunch supporter of the ruling party; privately, he supports all parties with occasional contributions towards their funds.[24]

Apart from these short paragraphs full of humour, there are a number of humorous situations and episodes. Ganpat's story of the ghost Bippin covers four pages of *Delhi is Not Far*. We burst into laughter at the end of the story. In the middle, too, we are amused and we smile at every turn. Similarly, the chapter "Rum and Curry" in *Vagrants in the Valley* is a humorous episode. Ram Singh's behaviour evokes laughter. At first he does not allow Sudheer and Rusty to enter his house. Later on, he allows them when he is told that they are government officers. He says that there is nothing to eat but when he sees that they have rum to drink, he brings pumpkins and potatoes and some spice to prepare curry to be taken with rum. They drink. At midnight Ram Singh pretends to be seriously ill and he is cured when he is given the medicine (the remaining rum in the bottle).

Sudheer's joke with Ram Singh about his bride is equally humorous.

Bond's humour adds savour to the stories of his novels. The short stories are compact and neatly structured. He seldom uses an archaic or uncommon word. The flow of reading is quite smooth. He can be favourably compared with R.K. Narayan as a storyteller. He may be named the Ancient Mariner; the mariner almost hypnotised the bridegroom by his story in Coleridge's famous poem "The Rime of the Ancient Mariner."

NOTES

1. *Rain in the Mountains*, 242-43.
2. Aldous Huxley, *Music at Night* (London: Penguin, 1931), 17.
3. E.M. Forster, *Aspects of the Novel* (London: Penguin, 1928, 1996), 87.
4. *Ruskin Bond: Collected Fiction*, 545.
5. Viktor Shklovsky, "Art as Technique", *Modern Criticism and Theory*, ed. David Lodge (London: Longman, 1988), 20.
6. *Ibid.*, 20*n*.
7. *Ibid.*, 21.

8. *Ruskin Bond: Complete Fiction*, 664.
9. *Ibid.*, 902.
10. *Ibid.*, 765.
11. E.M. Forster, *Aspects of the Novel*, 73.
12. *Ruskin Bond: Collected Fiction*, 545.
13. *Ibid.*, 572.
14. *Ibid.*, 630.
15. *Ibid.*, 896.
16. E.M. Forster, *Aspects of the Novel* (London: Penguin, 1928, 1996), 72.
17. David Lodge, *Working with Structuralism* (London: Longman, 1986), 2-5.
18. Roland Barthes, "Poe's Valdimar", *Modern Criticism and Theory*, David Lodge, ed. (London: Longman, 1988), 176.
19. *Ruskin Bond: Collected Fiction*, 946.
20. *Ibid.*, 641.
21. *Ibid.*, 742.
22. *Ibid.*, 696.
23. *Ibid.*, 766.
24. *Ibid.*, 769.

Conclusion

Ruskin Bond is one of the foremost novelists who have dealt with the adolescent life in Indian English literature. Born in an Anglo-Indian family and deprived of his parents at an early age (his mother divorced her father when Bond was about eight years old and father died when he was still at school) he faced the stern realities of life. Like Dickens he experienced the problems of a teenager who is left alone without parental support in this dark and wide world. He was lucky to get financial help to go to England to be a writer.

But inspite of the early success of the publication of *The Room on the Roof,* he found that England was not the place where he would be successful in life. Like Sir Ronald Ross, he longed for the sunny climate of India and the warm company of his friends in Dehradun.

His first three novels—*The Room on the Roof, Vagrants in the Valley* and *Delhi is Not Far*—are autobiographical. As has been shown in the preceding chapters, he has not changed the names of his friends like Somi, Chotu, Kishen and Ranbir in *The Room on the Roof.* Kishen remains the same in *Vagrants in the Valley.* It is only in *Delhi is Not Far* that we find all the names changed. However, the real figures lurking behind the imaginary are obviously visible.

The novels attract us not for the reason that they throw light on Bond's life but because they faithfully depict the emotions, behavioural pattern and thought-process of the adolescents.

The Room on the Roof is the story of an Anglo-Indian adolescent, Rusty, who has lost his parents and is left alone in a world where he has no relative to support him. His first encounter is with his guardian, Mr. Harrison, who is almost a tyrant and who chokes his natural growth. An adolescent is different from a child. A child is entirely dependent on its parents or guardian. It can protest but is unable to revolt. Harrison is unaware of this fact. Rusty, now an adolescent, is a changed boy. He wants independence and freedom to mix with the people of his choice. When he is physically assaulted, he revolts; he retaliates and beats Harrison severely. His encounter makes him realise that he has grown up and is now a young man. The two facts of adolescents we realise here. They are the adolescent's entrance to the world of the grown up people and the ability of self-assertion.

It is the self-assertion and the sense of having grown up that emboldens Rusty to leave his guardian's house and go to his friend's house to seek his future. Thirdly, the sense of having grown up manifests in his love for Meena Kapoor and the role of being a guardian of Kishen. Bond has stated these facts, not in terms of psychology or sociology but through the structure of the novel. The room is the symbol of the adolescent world.

Vagrants in the Valley is a novel about the untrammelled freedom of adolescents. They are all poor and live in abject poverty. They struggle for livelihood, eat poor food and yet are seldom unhappy. This depiction of the lower stratum of the Indian society is rare in Indian English literature. R.K. Narayan, Raja Rao, Bhabani Bhattacharya and Nayantara Sehgal are novelists of the middle class. Mulk Raj Anand, although a novelist with full sympathy with the lower class, does not identify himself with them. At best, he is a spokesman of the down-trodden class. The rest of the Indian English novelists write about the upper middle class and the upper class. Of course, Kamala Markandaya's *Nector in a Sieve* is an exception. Bond is not an onlooker; he is a part of the lower class. Rusty's position is not very much different from his friends. He is slightly better than goonga and Sudheer but poorer than the orphan Kishen who, later on, gets support from his relatives.

Rusty's journey to his aunt and to the house of Bhim is full of adventures. We must admire his fortitude and stamina. Rusty's ambition to be a writer is unquenchable despite his poverty. The other two female characters, Hastini and Mrinalini, come from the redlight area. Bond describes their life with accuracy. These women are sex workers and they have sex for their living but at heart they love Sudheer, the loafer. She dilapidated old church building, like the room in the preceding novel, is the world of the adolescents.

Delhi is Not Far is Bond's third autobiographical novel. Although the protagonist's name is not given in the novel, we easily recognize him that he is Rusty of the previous novels. Now, a young man crossing the border of adolescence, the protagonist becomes a protector of Suraj, a young boy studying in a school and earning his living by selling combs, buttons and other titbits. The protagonist saves Suraj's life when he is lying unconscious by the stroke of epilepsy. It is his company that Suraj's condition improves and the bouts of epilepsy become less frequent and, later on, very rare. The protagonist, like all aspiring creative writers, lives in penury and is always in debt. He lives among the people of low income and develops friendship with Kamla, a sex worker. It is by dint of his labour, he gets an appointment in a Delhi based publishing house. His fortune now rises and Delhi which seemed to be very far is now reached. Delhi, of course, is the symbol of success and the room on the roof is the symbol of the adolescent's world.

A Flight of Pigeons is the story of an Anglo-Indian girl and her family. The family's fortune crashes when Mr. Labadoor, a clerk in the British government, is killed in the violence of the 1857 war of independence. The author is more concerned with the humanity of the middle class families which did not hate Ruth, Mariam and other members of the family. On the other hand, the family is protected in the heat of the trouble. What is significant is that the entire story is narrated by the adolescent girl Ruth. The novelist's achievement lies in his depiction of the Muslim families in their day today life. We must admire Bond's keen observation of the interiors of Muslim houses.

Bond is an immaculate short-story writer. His short stories have simple plots and they all can be read in a single sitting. The four short-stories that are analysed in this book are thematically related. The girl and the narrator both are adolescents in "Night Train at Deoli". It is quite normal for an adolescent to fall in love with a pretty young girl. In this story the narrator, a college student, is charmed by the beauty and innocence of a young basket-selling girl. His love remains unrequited as the girl refuses to go with him to Delhi. But he hopes in vain to see her at the platform whenever the train stops at Deoli. Madhu is the other adolescent girl. The narrator helps her with books and regular teaching. She falls in love with him when she reaches thirteen. As there is a great age difference, the narrator has no idea of her love. It is only when she is asked to go to a boarding school to study that her love for him is revealed. She falls seriously ill and dies. "Love is a Sad Song" is the story of an adult who has fallen in love with a young girl of sixteen. It is the physical change in Sushila at the age of sixteen that entices the narrator. They have sexual contact but marriage does not take place. The reasons given by Sushila's family and her own reason are flimsy but strong enough to frustrate the possibility of marriage. "Time Stops at Shamli" is the sequel of "Love is a Sad Song." The narrator meets Sushila, now married to Mr. Dayal, at Shamli. Sushila loves him and promises to love him but will not go with him. Thus all the stories are of unrequited love.

Bond's technique and style are original. All his novels and short stories have their location in the Garhwal region of present day Uttaranchal. We all know hills and valleys have their own charm. The lush green forests, the blue hills and the smiling hill people all charm the people from the plains. Bond, as it is evident from his book *Rains in the Mountain,* is a great lover of nature. In fact, he found it difficult for him to resist the call of the Himalayas and the people of Garhwal (especially Dehra) while he was in England. All his novels and short stories depict the Himalayan beauty. The flora and fauna of Garhwal are painted in their full splendour.

Bond begins his short-stories and novels in a way which leads us to an exotic and romantic world. His technique illustrates Viktor Shklovsky's concept of defamiliarization. He seldom names the important characters in the beginning. We come to know Rusty's name at the end of the first chapter of *The Room on the Roof*. Similarly, the world of "Time Stops at Shamli" is a strange world and so are the characters. In fact, it is a story which we never forget and yet want to read it again.

In the art of narration he has very few equals and his place as a short-story writer of children and novelist of the adolescents in secure in Indian English literature.

Select Bibliography

Ruskin Bond's Books

Collected Fiction. New Delhi: Penguin, 1996.

Rain in the Mountains. New Delhi: Penguin, 1993.

Scenes from a Writer's Life. New Delhi: Penguin, 1997.

Critical Books

Singh, Prabhat Kumar. Ed. *Creative Contours of Ruskin Bond*. New Delhi: Pencraft, 1995.

There are a few articles and reviews published in *The Times of India* and *The Hindu* but they are all journalistic and encomiastic. Most of the literature on Bond is related to interviews and reminiscences.